VIBES FROM THE OTHER SIDE

vibes
from the
other
side

ACCESSING YOUR SPIRIT GUIDES
& OTHER BEINGS FROM THE BEYOND

catharine allan

STERLING ETHOS

New York

STERLING ETHOS
New York

ISBN 978-1-4549-4450-8
ISBN 978-1-4549-4451-5 (e-book)

For information about custom editions, special sales, and premium
purchases, please contact specialsales@unionsquareandco.com.

Manufactured in Canada

2 4 6 8 10 9 7 5 3 1

unionsquareandco.com

Image credits: Shutterstock.com: Alexey Boldin (ombre);
HorenkO (sunbeams); maybealice (icons)

Cover design by Melissa Farris
Interior design by Raphael Geroni

To all those whose gifts are
misunderstood and dismissed,
I see you.

Contents

PART 1. What Is a Medium?

PART 2. Connecting to the Other Side

PART 3. All Manner of Spirits

PART 4. Spiritual Protection

PART 5. Grounding It into Daily Life

Introduction

VIBES FROM THE OTHER SIDE. WHAT DOES THAT really mean? I believe that in everyone's life, there is some form of spirit contact. For many, it will happen once in a lifetime. It could be during a painful event, such as when a parent passes, or after a frightening medical diagnosis, or sometimes more happily with the birth of a child. The veils are pierced for that split second, and suddenly almost everyone around can perceive the spiritual realm and feel a contact. When it's a once-in-a-lifetime event, many will attribute it to their higher power, whatever that is—but others will identify it as the presence of a spirit.

Other people will encounter the spirit realm frequently, feeling that they live half on Earth and half in a separate plane. But in both instances, it is crucial to be able to discern what to pay attention to, how to understand the ways in which Spirit communicates, know when that communication is real, and decide when integrating these messages into our lives is beneficial to our well-being. In this book, I will do my best to share what I have learned about distinguishing spirit contact and integrating it into daily life, and help you understand how to do that too.

From my experience, there are as many varieties of spirits as there are beings on the planet. Some are angelic; some are a higher power or deity; some are ancestors. Some are people who walked the Earth who you've never met; some are interdimensional beings; some are animal totems—animals that come to you as guides, or even our pets (past, present, and future). All are valid.

Some types of spirits that we encounter can also be of a lower nature—beings that do not know they are dead—ghosts and entities, beings that are stuck or trapped, in pain or terribly angry. Sometimes we can encounter things that aren't from this world—you can call them evil or malevolent. Beings of the brightest light exist, and the darkest beings also exist. That is the nature of the universe, and you feel it most intimately when you are a medium.

I will help you understand the range of these experiences and beings and connect to those that resonate with you the most. I will help you spiritually protect yourself and ground your practice in everyday life. I have so many beautiful experiences to share with you to give you strength and hope.

Let's begin.

"You are not your body; you are not your
brain, not even your mind.
You are Spirit. All you have to do is
reawaken to the memory, to remember."

....

—DR. BRIAN WEISS

Part 1

....

What Is a Medium?

"Looking for consciousness in the brain is like looking inside a radio for the announcer."

— NASSIM HARAMEIN

W HAT IS THE MYSTERIOUS ART OF mediumship? How can we reach out to the energies of the spiritual realm, and how can we make ourselves receptive to its messages? Is communication with the souls or energies of a loved one who has passed, or a companion spirit guide, something we can all experience? The answer is yes, and I am about to show you how.

CHAPTER 1

Understanding Mediumship

I T IS A FUNCTION OF OUR MOST PRIMAL CURIOSITY to ask, "Is this all there is?" Many people across space and time have wondered whether their most surface-level daily interactions, thoughts, and feelings represent the full spectrum of human consciousness. It was the question of whether there is more that has led us to what we would now call mediumship.

What is mediumship? At its most basic, mediumship is an attempt to communicate with that "something more." A common reason is that we want to communicate with loved ones who have passed on and know that they are okay. Often we want to give them a message: that we have forgiven them. We want to ask a question: Are we forgiven? Often this means that we are also looking for proof of an afterlife—proof that the very essence of us survives physical death. Our belief in a lasting soul or spirit, whether it ultimately rests in another world or leads to our journey into reincarnation, can affect our whole belief system, our paradigm, the choices we make to live. All are profoundly affected by how we see life and death, the existence of a soul, the belief in an afterlife or nothingness. If there is a Creator of this universe, what is he, she, or it like? If you believe in spirits, souls, gods, goddesses, angels, or any of the other entities I cover in this book, then you may live your life with the desire to keep your own soul protected and to communicate with the other souls that exist in this world and the next. That desire is at the root of mediumship. This practice is not for everyone, and that's okay. I respect all beliefs that do not cause harm or take away people's rights. But if you're curious about how to reach out and want to know what guidance you can derive from that connection, read on!

From my experience, the belief that we do have a soul and that it lives on after death is an enormous comfort and a valuable guide in life. It brings a richness to our lives and gives much-needed psychological closure and relief of suffering. When the spirit of a loved one, an ancestor, a being of light (Archangels or sometimes your deceased ancestors), a pet, an animal totem (an animal that comes to you in person or a dream that is highly symbolic at the time and helps you), an angel, or an ascended master such as Buddha, Jesus, or other Spiritual Teachers and Leaders who have lived on Earth but went through profound spiritual transformations and are available for us to call upon— comes through to speak to you and that voice is authentic, the relief that will be experienced by you and even the spirits you are speaking to is palpable. A medium is one who can communicate with all manner of spirit forms and relay their messages to others with compassion and integrity. Anyone can use these techniques.

Many people wonder if anyone can become a medium. I see that almost everyone can and will have an experience of mediumship in their lives, usually when there is a death in the family or an event that shakes us up. Mystical experiences and abilities are in all of us, but many of us aren't going to access them as a regular practice. It may be a breakthrough event once in a lifetime, or several times, and this is very common. To be a true medium means that you have opened your psyche up enough to receive the spirit world on a regular basis. Many of us are capable of this, but not many of us want to or can handle it emotionally. It is akin to waking up one day and suddenly speaking a new language, having all new family and friends to speak with, but possibly losing the bonds of others who don't understand your new language.

There are many types of mediums. Much of the history of mediumship explores the survival of the soul beyond physical death on a research level, and there have been many books published on the subject, starting in Victorian times. These studies and experiences have always been fascinating, yet they have also been contested throughout history. It is no small thing to change your belief system, nor do you have to! If I had not had direct experience with it, I might also have remained skeptical or unwilling to adopt it as a core truth of life. I hope to help you discern some of your own experiences or inclinations so you will be able to trust your direct experiences as well. As the astute psychiatrist-turned-past-life-regressionist Dr. Brian Weiss puts it, "Experience is stronger than belief. Once we have experiences, our mind begins to open. This works better than me forcing my own experience or knowledge onto anyone. Show them how to have their own experiences." This book is a guide that will help you have your own experiences, and whether they convince you is your own choice.

What Can a Medium Do?

This is the million-dollar question, isn't it? Most discussions of spirit contact seem to be about whether this communication is real or not. History has had both its true mediums and its tricksters. For example, in the early twentieth century, American "medium" Abraham Hochman claimed to specialize in finding missing husbands—which was considered a social epidemic at the time. A Yiddish newspaper in New York City published a "Gallery of Missing Husbands" in 1909, when it was thought that as many as 31,000 men had abandoned their duties as husbands and fathers in very tough economic times. Hochman offered his services to those obsessed with finding these men; but in reality his interests were more in hosting lavish parties and taking the money of the desperate people who hired him. As *Atlas Obscura* reported, "A 1909 *New York Times* article estimated that $10,000 a day was paid to some 1,000 fortune tellers of all cultures at a time when a simple reading typically costs 15 cents and cautioned that 'the opportunities of the unprincipled person to prey on the ignorance and pathetic truthfulness of these believers in the occult is almost limitless.'" This same fear has persisted into the present day.

Anyone in a vulnerable position who seeks an expert is, in a way, at their mercy. It happens all the time when we need a doctor, lawyer, or police officer to help us. We all know that just because a person has a position of authority doesn't mean that they have perfect ethics, but we give that basic consent and trust. When people come to see a medium or clairvoyant, they are usually very vulnerable. In the early twentieth century, mediumship wasn't regulated at all; and even now it can be difficult to know who is qualified or have recourse when you've been swindled. It has at least gotten easier to protect your-self since Hochman's time. By 1911, bilking people out of money in exchange for claims of finding missing persons had become all but illegal. Law enforcement clamped down on certain kinds of psychics in the tenements of New York City. And yet, in spite of laws protecting the citizenry against this kind of predatory behavior, there is still plenty of suspicion against tricksters masquerading as genuine mediums.

If you want to develop your own mediumship abilities, you defi-nitely can, and I will show you some ways to connect here in later sections. However, if you decide to consult a medium, there are some things to know. A good medium, someone true to their gift and authen-tic in their readings, will understand the nature of Spirit. When the medium is real, they will be able to give you detailed information on the kinds of spirits that you are encountering. Although these details aren't always revealed in a dramatic, Hollywood-style way, a real medium will give you sensitive, useful information. Real mediums are not like a jukebox where you press the button and it speed-dials someone's soul and they spit out the answer you want to hear, but they do have amazing abilities that can help you understand the spiritual realm—and they may even be useful to you if you'd like to develop your own abilities.

Take communicating with the spirit of someone who has passed on. The soul who has crossed over is often in a sleepy state of mind—if their death was traumatic, they may still be processing it and may not be ready to talk about it yet; or they may not have fully crossed over and processed their transition; or they may simply be resting after a life fully lived. The range and variety of states of presence that our loved ones are in when they cross over is just as vast as down here on Earth. There is no instant-angel button to press to get the answers you seek. Some souls go straight to the light right away and will communicate freely and share their wisdom quickly, but this is rare. Many will go to the light as if there is a big party happening over there and, without a second look at the life on Earth they've left, are happy to rejoin other souls they know—who are often not family in this life. Lots of folks on Earth feel disappointed when they hear about this behavior. They want to feel as if their loved ones are compelled to stick around and watch over them. And while many spirits do linger and watch over you in your life in certain ways, they may not provide concrete directions about what to do at every twist and turn. But, regardless, they are there, and they feel for you and will give you signs or appear during the most trying times of your life.

Many who cross over do not feel like, or are even concerned with, watching over anyone. They are busy with the progress of their own soul and the lessons they are learning. It does not mean they never loved us. If someone is busy studying for a huge exam and cannot go out or talk for a while, do you tell yourself they don't love you anymore? Of course not. You know they are busy doing important work for themselves, and this is also true for many souls.

We must talk about difficult topics to be real. If a medium tells you fairy tales about your loved ones that never vary from one account to the next, they are just regurgitating what they know people want to hear. A true medium will be able to tell you if the spirit you seek isn't there, isn't ready, is "sleeping," has not crossed over yet due to a tragic or traumatic death, or something else. If the narrative you get from a medium is always an easy feel-good one, it's not real.

This is all to say that when you yourself reach out to spirits, you need to understand that you may not get the answers you wanted. However, if you open yourself up to the variety of communication you may receive, you will benefit from a wealth of knowledge in the world beyond this one. It's best to learn how to communicate with spirits yourself, trusting your intuition, being open and aware of the signs you are given, mindful of the patterns that appear when you think of a lost loved one, paying attention to your dreams. In this book we'll discuss all of those techniques and more, and hopefully will give you a solid foundation for beginning your own journey into reaching out to the other side.

History of Mediumship and Spirit Communication

There have been mystics, sages, and other spirit communicators throughout the world for centuries. It is an inherent part of the human experience to seek—and sometimes touch—the Divine. As human consciousness evolved, the capacity to perceive beyond the tangible realm—beyond the instinct or intuition we evolved as a species also developed. Mediumship is a universally human perceptual experience that has been evolving for millennia. This overview of its history will hopefully give you a strong sense of its importance in our evolution. Of course, this does not include the many mediums, shamans, and seers who went under the radar practicing these arts in secret sacred spaces or on anonymous kitchen tables, let alone the volume of personal experiences that may only be written in a diary, told to a trusted confidant, or simply went to the grave with the people who experienced them.

When we speak of mediumship in modern times, we usually think of the Long Island Medium or John Edward communicating with a grandmother who has passed in front of a live audience and/

or a television camera. However, mediumship—communication with the spirits—is as old as time and includes awareness and rituals on a broader scale than just contacting an individual who has passed on.

Celtic Paganism, on which we base our modern Halloween, is a ritual of recognition that the veils between the spirit world and ours are thinner at that time of year, and so enable us to feel their presence more. We give out food or candy and hang herbs on the front door, all to appease these spirits and protect us from evil. Versions of this practice exist in indigenous tradition all over the world. It might be a different god or deity; a different spiritual holiday; a different herb or food, dance, or walk; but indigenous practices based on spirit communication are global. People have long believed that certain spiritual beings can influence daily life, so they created ceremonies and rituals to communicate with them. These are often rituals to encourage or appease the spirits to make crops grow, to bless a village with rain, and sometimes to protect them from harm (for example, the evil eye). Sometimes they're just generalized techniques to cultivate good fortune. We could regard this as archaic or quaint, but really it's not. Plenty of people still practice them or derivatives of them all over the world today. Just ask your grandparents.

In ancient Greece circa 1400 BCE, the Oracle of Delphi channeled messages to crowds of people who made the pilgrimage to see her. Communication rituals have existed in China, Tibet, and New Zealand—just to name a few—for centuries. There are also Spiritualist traditions all over the world—that is, the belief that the spirits of the deceased are not static and live on, are able to communicate with us, and have a desire to do so. There are many Spiritualist churches alive and operating today. It's impossible to mention every culture and country without writing a thesis, but I want to show you some very interesting examples in history.

To start out, let's take a closer look at the Oracle of Delphi. People traveled for days to hear the Oracle speak. Imagine yourself walking for five days straight with no camping gear, just to potentially hear a message from a spirit or guidance on your life path. The Oracles were considered to be anointed with the sun-god Apollo's gifts of sight, which enabled them to channel messages from him.

In ancient China, *Tongji* channeled the energies of spirits in a similar way. The term for a Chinese folk religious practitioner, *Tongji* (童乩) is often translated as "spirit medium." Said to have been chosen by a god or spirit, a *shen* (神), as an earthly vehicle for divine expression, a Tongji is different than a *wu* (巫), or shaman, who gains control of forces in the spirit world for the purposes of healing, as opposed to a Tongji, who appears to be entirely under their control.

The Chinese still practice rituals of spirit communication, a five-thousand-year-old practice that is widespread and also extends to Taiwan and Southeast Asia. They are part of the indigenous religion of China, which has existed, in the words of renowned anthropologist Professor J. J. M. de Groot, "since even before the dawn of time." These rituals can be traced back to the Neolithic era, which tells us something about the practice's magnetic power.

In the Maori tradition, the medium was called a *tohunga*, meaning "expert" or "appointed one." Spirits would communicate through the tohunga, whose voice would change as the spirit entered them. This was regarded as the voice of the god, and the person who spoke in this tone was *a waka atua* or *kauwaka*, or "vessel of a god."

Most indigenous practices across the world include some form of healer or shaman, channeler, seer, or medium. Therefore, I believe it is part of our human conscious evolution. They may be found in a small village and given offerings of food and shelter in order to spiritually guide the people there or to foresee events in the future for their protection. Mediums and seers were also a part of courtly life in many places. They moved from the mouthpiece of the gods to the adviser to the king—or, in the next example, as the trance channel for the Dalai Lama. Tibetan Buddhism includes a unique mixture of Buddhism, Indian Buddhism, and Tantric traditions. A major difference between Tibetan Buddhism and Buddhism outside Tibet is the belief in a soul. As Martha Meilleur writes, "When Buddhism came to Tibet in the mid-8th century AD/CE, it brought with it many deities which had evolved from the gods of Hinduism, but it also 'converted' a great many of the original Tibetan shamanic spirits to Buddhist and bound them by oath to be defenders of Buddhism and its teachings." In the seventeenth century, the 5th Dalai Lama appointed a State Oracle (*Nechung*), who played a huge political role, advising and giving messages. The Nechung, while entranced, participated in ceremonies in which he would channel guidance from the spirit realm to advise the Dalai Lama or other government officials, and sometimes also answered questions and provided guidance to others, such as aristocratic families.

In Britain and the United States, the 1840s brought with them a rise in the popularity of séances. With the increased interest in the spirit realm during the Victorian era and early twentieth century, people with actual gifts—as well as others who were proven to be tricksters—emerged. The stereotypes that proliferated during that era are still with us today—people dressed up in their best, sitting around fancy Victorian tables with their hands upon a beautiful linen tablecloth, awaiting the spirit of a dearly departed person to appear. It's a whole aesthetic now, but it was very real and practiced widely at the time. From that time in history, we get our imagery of Ouija boards, people fainting and going into trances, and people up on stages giving displays of spirit communications or speaking messages to an audience under a tent.

In the time between the mid-1800s and the mid-1900s, mediums and séances were all the rage. Plenty of celebrities of the day, from political figures like Andrew Jackson Davis, spiritual leaders like Helena Petrovna Blavatsky, and cultural and artistic heroes like Arthur Conan Doyle became fascinated and participated in Spiritualism-focused events. The White House even hosted a séance, and it wasn't uncommon for them to be held in the homes of the rich and well-regarded.

One infamous pair of mediums who sparked a lot of interest and then controversy at the time were the Fox Sisters. They said they had solved a crime by channeling a spirit. They used the now-cliché technique of rapping on a wall to indicate answers from Spirit while mesmerizing their audiences. It must have been very impressive and creepy back in the day, but sadly the sisters were exposed as frauds in 1888. The hype the sisters got, versus the disappointment and sense of betrayal that people felt, set off another trend of testing and examining mediums to make sure they were real. Some mediums were exposed, but many people were converted from skeptics to believers. In some cases, the skeptic became a medium, such as Dr. Robert Hare, who first set out to prove that mediumship was a fraud , and through investigation came to decide that it was real and became a medium himself!

Another significant figure in the history of mediumship at the time was Alan Kardec. Kardec coined the term Spiritualism around 1860 in his book *Spiritist Codification*. In 1884, he founded the College of Psychic Studies, which opened its doors in London, England. It is still going strong. At one point in 1925, it was headed by Sir Arthur Conan Doyle. Another prominent school founded to study and develop psychic abilities was Stanstead Hall, founded by Arthur Findlay in Essex dating back to 1871. Stanstead Hall became a school in 1964, just before he died; but before then it was used by the Spiritualists' National Union. Finally, it's impossible to mention the development and research of mediumship in the West without mentioning Edgar Cayce, who was known as "the sleeping prophet" because he would channel messages in his dreams. He founded the ARE, or Association for Research and Enlightenment, in 1937 in Virginia Beach, Virginia. All these institutions are still open to this day for courses in person or online and include support and mentorship. The schools in the UK even offer accreditation, which is something that doesn't exist in North America—though it should!

I hope this very brief overview impresses upon you how long humans have been communing with Spirit, be it through a medium or through cultural rituals, for messages from the Divine, from an ancestor or general prayer, or appeasing to the gods. I think it is part of our DNA to explore and receive guidance and support from Spirit.

CHAPTER 2

Types of Mediumship

THERE ARE A FEW TYPES OF MEDIUMSHIP: mental, physical, and trance. The following sections break down the distinctions between these groups a bit.

One note, though: just remember that a psychic isn't necessarily a medium, but a medium *is* a psychic. As Rebecca Rosen wrote in an article on *Oprah Daily,* "Psychics tune into the energy of people or objects by feeling or sensing elements of their past, present, and future. . . . A medium uses his or her psychic or intuitive abilities to see the past, present, and future events of a person by tuning in to the spirit energy surrounding that person." In other words, a medium is a person who speaks to those who have crossed over, as well as beings in other dimensions or realms, communicating with—or perceiving the presence of—an entity or a spirit guide, ascended master, or higher consciousness, including *all* realms.

Mental Mediumship

The Arthur Findlay College of Intuitive Sciences in Essex, England offers courses in healing, mediumship, trance healing, and trance mediumship, among others. According to them, "Mental mediumship ... occurs through the medium's own consciousness, without the use of the five physical senses." So that would mean connecting to spirits through the "Clairs": Clairvoyance (clear-seeing), Clairsentience (clear-sensing), Clairaudience (clear-hearing), Claircognizance (clear-thinking), Clairgustance (clear-tasting), and Clairalience (clear-smelling). These same Clairs are part of our intuitive system and can be developed by anyone—not just someone with above-average spirit-sensing abilities. Mental mediumship represents what we often think of as a clairvoyant, psychic, or intuitive reader. This is probably the most common form of mediumship and may be difficult to distinguish for outsiders, since they may not see physical evidence of the medium's connection to the spirits.

EXAMPLES OF MENTAL MEDIUMSHIP

Since this is the most common way that mediums function, I want to give you a good sense of how this happens, in case you recognize it in yourself or others you know. Mental mediumship is receiving the spirit contact through the Clairs, through the mind. An example of this would be waking up one morning and getting a flash visual of your cat, who passed away last year. The spirit of your cat is there in the room, but the way it comes is a mental-image flash. Another example could be that you are taking a long walk in the forest, and you hear your name being called. When you stop and identify the quality of this voice, it feels like either a relative who passed away or a fairy or deity calling your name. You hear this name in your head, not literally out loud for others to hear. These would both be mental mediumship, and it's a pretty common phenomenon for us to experience when we trust our intuition and strengthen our mindfulness. You might have noticed that both of these examples are at times when you'd be calmer and more likely to contact your intuitive side.

Physical Mediumship

Physical mediumship "can be defined as manipulation of energies and energy systems by spirit discarnate. This type of mediumship involves manifestations, such as loud raps and noises, voices (through direct voice), materialized objects such as apports, transfiguration (where clear spirit faces appear in front of the medium's face), materialized spirit bodies, or body parts such as hands, legs, and feet." When physical mediumship happens, everyone can see the manifestation of the spirit or hear the raps or noises, regardless of whether they are psychic or not. The word *physical* means it has manifested as a tangible, audible, and visible phenomenon or communication.

One form of physical mediumship is evidential spiritual mediumship. This type of medium will work both as a physical and mental medium, often at the same time. I find that this is the form most people want to practice, perhaps because they feel that by producing this kind of evidence which confirms that spirits are real, they can be sure of their messages. However, I find that this level of spirit interaction is actually quite terrifying at times, and messages often seem to come from those spirits who are stuck in this Earth realm—not quite the beings of light from whom we often long to hear. In my own experience, if there is a physical manifestation of a spirit, it is often stuck between realms instead of in the light, and therefore it might be heavier energy, not as easy to deal with.

EXAMPLES OF PHYSICAL MEDIUMSHIP

This was the type of mediumship practiced by the infamous Fox Sisters. In their séances, they often employed a system of raps on a wall, which meant the channeled spirit was saying "yes" or "no." While this is representative of a real phenomenon, the actual experience of physical mediumship isn't as literal as an instant ask and answer. An example might be that you move into a new home and hear noises in the basement even though no one is there—no person or squirrel or pet has made this noise. It's very common for spirits to stay in their former homes and either be seen walking around, or be heard rustling around or closing a door or window. Does this mean that the home is haunted? Well, yes. Here's the thing, though: some spirits are nice and people feel comforted having them there, and others are not happy and create disturbances. So, if engaging in physical mediumship, you won't be asking them direct questions and expecting to hear an answer, but the spirit will be audible or visible to those who live there. This happened to cousins of mine who lived in a home that was a former War of 1812 hospital and part of the Underground Railroad. The whole family has heard or seen spirits in the house for years. They just wouldn't engage in a question-and-answer session if prompted.

Another example you might experience is to see your favorite dog, who has passed, running around your yard. You might feel him jump into the bed where he used to sleep, even though he crossed over many years ago. So many people have told me stories like this that I never doubt it. If you hear your former dog barking, and others have heard them too, or if you feel a depression in the bedcovers as you fall asleep one night, their spirit is there with you physically.

Trance Mediumship

What is a trance, exactly? We can say it is a "temporary mental condition in which someone is not completely conscious of and/or not in control of him or herself" as it is defined in the *Cambridge Dictionary*. We can all go into a trance at times. With practice and lots of meditation, people can enter into deeper states of trance where the focus is so inward and connected to the subconscious that they can access sides of themselves and knowledge they wouldn't as easily be able to when awake. People go into trances for hypnosis work, and of course mediums enter into trances to speak deeply with Spirit. So how is this any different than mental mediumship? You could be doing anything in daily life, and mental mediumship can still take place. You can be washing the dishes and—*flash!*—a person or spiritual being appears suddenly in your mind. For trances, that just won't fly. Think of a hypnotic state, a semi-sleeping state, a very deep state of relaxation where you are so in touch with every personal feeling and sensation. You are not in your head—you are fully in your body, and you are in a state of surrender. People get scared or nervous at that, because it's a vulnerable state. However, we can't receive information on this level if we aren't fully open and vulnerable. A good trance medium knows how to put him or herself into this trance in order to receive spiritual communication from any source.

Once a medium is in a trance, a spirit or entity can speak or gesture through the medium's body. Teaching and healing can then occur, and those lessons are often very powerful. I will be sharing more of these stories from my life's work in upcoming chapters. There are many examples of famous mediums who were in trance to transmit information from a specific being, like the classic book *Seth Speaks*. In *Seth Speaks*, we learn about Jane Roberts, who channeled the being called Seth, whose imparted wisdom has since been written into a few novels. Edgar Cayce was also a trance medium. As a preteen, Cayce channeled spiritual knowledge from his schoolbooks, and then later went on to give psychic readings. Later still, he was able to give healings in a trance state. He was often referred to as "the sleeping prophet" for this reason.

A more recent example of a trance medium would be Esther Hicks, who channels wisdom from a being called Abraham, and has done so for the past thirty years or so in her seminars. The energy shift in her as she delivers his messages is palpable. I have also seen with my own eyes a local well-known medium named Marilyn Rossner in Montreal who hosted circles and services at her Spiritualist church. I witnessed spirits entering her body on more than one occasion. Trance states take a high level of skill to allow, to manage energetically and emotionally, and to return and recover from. Otherwise, we would call this a possession! Mediumship isn't for sissies—it's not a party trick or a joke.

EXAMPLES OF TRANCE MEDIUMSHIP

A perfect example of this goes back to the book by Dr. Brian Weiss, *Many Lives, Many Masters*. In the accounts he writes about in this book, his subject was undergoing hypnosis to heal a personal issue and started to channel her own past lives, but she also channeled the child that Brian lost. She was in such a deep hypnotic state that she was receptive to the spirit of his child around him and delivered messages. You might have an experience of trance mediumship if you are doing hypnosis, but it might even happen when you are very relaxed during a massage. It could happen when you are in that semi-conscious state when you are about to fall asleep or just about to wake up. During these times, your mental guard is down and you are open to sensing anything around you.

My Story

When I was younger, I didn't know I was a medium at all. I did see spirits in my room when I was five, but they were animals and my family, so I didn't comprehend these experiences as "seeing a spirit" the way other kids might when they say there is a person in their room. I was always able to see through people to their true self, their true nature and feelings. People couldn't hide that from me, and I also remember having a strong connection to nature and a mystical sense of the world all my life—meaning I knew everything was alive and mysterious and wonderful. I only realized I was a medium when it spontaneously started to happen in my twenties.

To give you a bit of background on how I discovered I was a medium and how I determined what sort of medium I was, here's a bit of my personal story. I always knew I could see the truth behind what people didn't want to see or say, and I had begun to study astrology at the age of fifteen, and tarot at around twenty-two. I began giving tarot readings, but didn't know I was a medium right away. Then, in 1993, I was invited to give short tarot readings at a birthday party for a friend. I had only been reading my tarot at that point for about a year and hadn't done many professional readings yet, but I had worked for a telephone psychic line, and I did know I could give accurate readings, because I got feedback of my accuracy from everyone.

This was back in the first days of the telephone-hotline-style readings. At the time, I saw a want ad for a tarot reader in an alternative newspaper in Montreal called *The Mirror*. It's where you went back then to find an apartment, a good band or restaurant, a bit of news, and read the "Real Astrology" column by Rob Brezny. I answered the ad even though I was a bit intimidated, being so new at my readings, but the woman behind it, JZ Crystal, ended up auditioning me. I did a reading for her live in her living room so she could be sure I was real before I was hired. That's not done anymore, I can tell you!

When I started the job, I did readings by phone in a room with maybe thirty other psychics in a little apartment over a busy highway. I met mediums there, but still didn't know I was one myself. I knew my astrology and my tarot very well, but my spirit guides still weren't real to me, and my awareness that I could speak to the other side hadn't really dawned on me yet.

It wasn't until I was hired for that fateful birthday party that I knew a little more about my own abilities. The party organizers set me up beside a dance floor (which, in the future, I would realize was a big no-no—too noisy and zero privacy). A woman sat down, and I started to channel my cards, which is quite different from purely reading the cards. In those days, I found myself slipping into trance-like states and seeing things in the cards that had nothing to do with their classic meanings. The messages I got were more precise than a tarot alone can give you. Just for a bit of context, many people will learn or memorize the tarot and can give a very accurate reading from a more academic perspective. What I was doing was quite different. I was wide open energetically to the people sitting before me and was starting to receive images, words, and bodily feelings—I'd later recognize this as clairvoyance, clairaudience, and clairsentience. I was also starting to receive information in a download. Channeling feels like that. You spontaneously receive a block of information, and you tell the person what you are receiving. It comes very quickly and in precise detail and has nothing to do with the meanings of the tarot cards. So, my client drew the Three of Swords, a card illustrated by a heart stabbed by three swords in very dark colors. In my mind, an image flashed: the face of an individual, and then a wave of emotional pain. I told the woman in front of me that I felt a lot of loss around her and asked if she was okay. I looked up and she was crying. She told me that the face I had seen was her husband, and he had died about a year before. I did my best to comfort her, but in that setting it was very hard. People wanted things to be fun and entertaining, and I didn't have long with her before the next person came bouncing over to my table (another reason to have privacy while doing readings). I've never forgotten her face or that moment, because I'd sensed the death, and it was accurate. I did not channel her husband at that party, though. In other words, I saw her husband's image, and I felt her pain and knew it was a loss or sadness, but at that time I didn't have the experience to identify the fact that his spirit had passed, and that the sadness was her grief. The emotion could have been from another experience she had had, or one her husband had had while he was still alive.

Flash forward, and I began giving readings at a pagan shop called Le Melange Magique in downtown Montreal in 1997. Every so often, this same type of channeling during a reading would happen again. It was not happening enough for me to flag it until further into my career, and then it was very regular. At one point, I asked the staff what might be going on with me. I said, "Every time I start describing someone to them in detail, they tell me they've passed on." I explained that, for me, the spirits of the departed I sensed were as real as the energies of the living, still souls with quirks and things to say. Members of the pagan shop's staff answered me very casually, saying, "Oh, you are a medium, then." I said, "Am I?" And from that time on, I began to read up on it. Sure enough, all the experiences described in the books I read were things I had been living without knowing about mediumship or ever trying to perform it. The staff of the store also warned me to be careful, a lesson that didn't become clear until later when I began to feel confident in telling people what I was. That's when all manner of folks began to come to me with deep, gut-wrenching, and sometimes very creepy stories, and the lesson came with enormous expectation that I wasn't ready for. Still, although these experiences were initially very difficult, my predictions have been very accurate and have helped so many people that I feel confident in continuing my practice.

Becoming a Medium

Can anyone become a medium, you may wonder? I would say that anyone can if they are empathic and open to receive on this level. So I would say that many people will have at least one experience in a lifetime that spontaneously comes to them that is a spirit contact. Many people will disregard it, some will block it out of fear, some will be very touched, and it can shift the course of their lives. If you desire to open up to the spirit realm to feel and connect to your loved ones or spirit guides, it is a very enriching journey. I will use the rest of this book to help you break down different ways to open up and connect, protect your sacred space, process information you receive so that you'll know what to trust, and hopefully inspire you to experience a very meaningful side of your life.

Most of this book is about helping you connect on your own, even if you want to share your experiences with friends or family. This is largely an inner path, as opposed to more social practices like tarot readings or astrology that enable you to give readings to others. The first leg of the journey is all about connecting deeply to yourself and trusting yourself.

If you want to develop your skills more, perhaps you have already experienced much of what I will describe here and need to know further steps or how to use it in relation to get spiritual info for others. I can help you with this and train you. You can go to my website for all things related to this book at www.river-rain.com/vibes-from-the -other-side. The resources section in the back of the book also lists information for the two colleges operating now where you can develop your abilities and study them. I've also included a reading list of books by other authors that you may enjoy!

Part 2

....

Connecting to the Other Side

NOW THE JOURNEY BEGINS! I WILL take you through the many ways Spirit can speak to us, be it through loved ones, pets, or spirit guides. You will want to give yourself time to go through this section, do the accompanying exercises, and give yourself time to reflect and digest their results. It will seem simple and easy enough to read these sections, but engaging with them can be emotionally profound if you keep your mind and heart open and give yourself enough time to reflect on your experiences. You might want to keep a journal handy to write things down that come to mind or flash to you as I describe ways you can connect to Spirit yourself. You may have ideas already, and this section may inspire you to go deeper. Or you may be completely new to this and some of these exercises may awaken something in you. In any case, you don't want to miss any subtle bits of information that come to your awareness while reading this, so have something ready to record your process. You might want a box of tissues, too!

CHAPTER 3

Dreams

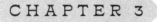

WHILE SOME PEOPLE WILL HAVE DIRECT encounters with spirits—perhaps see apparitions appear in their room or feel a touch—by far the most common experience of spirit communication is a dream encounter. Some dreams, just like anything, are a jumble of personal feelings you are resolving, and the dream is a mishmash. When it comes to these kinds of dreams, we can't truly say they are a spirit contact, even when you desperately desire them to be. However, when the dream feels very simple and strong, short and sweet, very often it's a contact.

Contact Dreams

So many dreams are complex, and we wake up feeling like they must mean something. Especially if it includes someone who passed or a being of some kind that seems to want to communicate, it's normal to think it could be a spiritual message to you from them. Sometimes that might be the case, but sometimes it's a dream where you're processing your emotions. Let's look at the difference.

DREAM #1

Sharon just quit her job and is wondering what is next in her career path. One night she has a dream that her great-aunt, who passed when Sharon was a child, is standing in her old workplace office with a box of cookies and tells her that this chapter is over in her life. She wakes up and feels that she's just had a distinct contact from her great-aunt, verifying that she made the right decision to leave that job. This dream is very strong and clear. It's simple, and she woke up feeling very affirmed. This dream is likely to represent a spirit contact.

DREAM #2

John is in the middle of a messy custody battle and has a dream that his kids are visiting his dad's house, even though he passed away a few years ago. In the dream, he drops off his kids at his dad's, and his current ex-wife answers the door. The house looks like his childhood home when he lived with his parents; but she is there, and her artwork is on the walls. He wakes up feeling overwhelmed and is not sure what this all means. He wonders if his dad is trying to give him a message. In this case, I would say this is likely *not* a spiritual contact dream, because it is too convoluted and represents several elements mixing between his childhood and his present. His ex-wife opening the door and her things being there would be more symbolic of her influence on him than a message from his dad talking about the artwork. There is no clear presence of his dad and no clear message from his dad in the dream.

DREAM #3

Cara wants to meet someone after having been single for a few years, and she meditates every night before bed, asking her spirit guides to show her in her dreams who she is meant to be with. One night, after many prayers for a sign, she has a dream of a man in a sailboat. The water is crystal-clear, and the light is very bright. The whole scenario is very calming and hopeful. She wakes up wondering if this is her future mate, or if the figure in her dream was a spirit guide. Or, she thinks, perhaps the dream was just a bit of hope in some form.

In this case, I would be inclined to say that the dream contained a spirit guide, because the scene felt so light, calm, and otherworldly, and brought Cara a sense of hope. It's possible that her future mate may have some of the qualities of the man in the boat, or he represents the kind of person she will meet, but he didn't step forward to give her any clear message. Spiritual contact with real people, as opposed to guides, tends to have a clear message that we can identify. If the man in the boat was wearing a shirt just like her great-grandfather wore, and her great-grandfather was also known for his love of the sea, then it could have been him in the dream. If the man in the boat seemed to have an otherworldly or dreamy feeling about him, and he spoke very gentle words or otherwise had body language meant to calm, and he had an aura of the ethereal—then he's most likely a spirit guide. And yes, sometimes it can be both: the great-grandfather is the spirit guide. If the man in the dream had been Cara's future mate coming to say hello, he would have indicated something to her about love, his arrival, or his personality, or otherwise something clear for her to watch for in the future.

Typical Spirit Contact Dreams from the Departed

The most common kind of dream encounter I hear about is one in which someone who has recently passed shows up in a dream saying they are okay, or they are with you acting as you normally remember them, and they are happy. This is usually straightforward: the dream is a confirmation that they are okay on the other side. Another common dream is of a loved one showing up to tell us something concrete that confirms their identity. Here's an example:

Julie had lost her mom about a year before her best friend Nancy had a very concrete dream of her presence. She dreamt that her mom was tapping on her kitchen window over and over. Nancy went to open the front door to say hello to her, and Julie's mom held up her wrist and said, "Look at my bracelet." Nancy wasn't sure why this was significant in the dream, so she said, "Okay, sure?" Julie's mom just kept saying, "Look at my bracelet" over and over again, continually holding it up for Nancy to see.

Later, Nancy told Julie her dream, after first saying, "I'm not crazy or smoking anything funny, but I had a dream about your mom last night." Julie was a bit nervous but told Nancy to go ahead and tell her about it. Nancy told Julie about the wrist and bracelet and Julie teared up. She said, "My mom died because she wasn't wearing her medic alert bracelet when she had a reaction to something she ate and went into diabetic shock." This was a crystal-clear sign to her that her mom's spirit was present in Nancy's dream, and that Julie's mother was telling them both that she was okay. The encounter even gave Julie a weird sense that her mom was apologizing for not wearing the bracelet. These kinds of dreams can definitely seem odd to us if we get them about people we don't know well, but if you feel safe enough to tell someone who was actually close to the person in your dream, you'll often hear beautiful stories like this that can help people a lot.

Sometimes the opposite is true: people can also dream of a spirit that appears to be upset. Keep in mind that these spirits are often transitioning between the living world and the next and are making peace with or digesting their life experiences. In this context, it makes sense that they are upset, and it may not mean anything more than that they are in flux, and it is scary and possibly difficult. Over time, you will probably dream of them again in a healthy and happy state as they progress in their soul's transition to the light.

To illustrate an example of this, I'll tell you about two of my cats who passed. My cat Gen had to be put to sleep at the age of eighteen due to kidney failure. Two days after she passed, I dreamed of her as the cuddly and active youngster she once had been. Gen seemed happy, and I knew her spirit was well. When my cat Chantal died—also an older cat of eighteen with kidney issues—she passed in the bathroom, alone. She came to me in dreams, clearly in distress, for two years before a good dream finally came. It is like this with humans, too. You can never say how long it might take for a person to process their life and transmute any negative emotions into positive. I hear many people say that these dreams happen for a few weeks or a couple of months after a person passes. For some, they won't have a dream for a year or more; for others, there won't be a dream at all. To clarify, this doesn't mean your departed loved ones aren't okay, or that they aren't going to show you signs of contact or reach out spiritually—it's just not going to be in the form of a dream.

Progression of the Soul
in Dreams

. . . .

Peter's mom died suddenly, and the whole family was in shock because she had hidden her cancer from everyone except her husband, his father. After her death, the father was dealing with his loss, but also with the secrecy and helplessness he felt because he hadn't had a chance to do anything for her. He began having dreams of her every night. She was always sitting in her favorite chair. Sometimes she looked sad, sometimes she wore black, sometimes she was smoking or drinking—which she had done a bit in real life. Every dream was bittersweet because she was there, but she didn't seem well or happy in any of them.

Over time, the father's dreams came less frequently, and he felt disappointed to lose the connection to her. Then one day he had an incredibly vivid dream. His wife was wearing a beautiful dress; she was younger, and her face and skin were vibrant. She pointed to something in the dream, her favorite tree. She indicated to him that he should go sit there and think of her. He woke up feeling hopeful and visited by her, finally. He went to that tree and sat there and felt her presence. All was well. After that, he felt her with him.

Sometimes your spirit guide will come in a dream to tell you that a loved one is now okay as well. This usually means the person's spirit is still processing their life—they have a vibe of someone in a deep sleep. For example, when Steven's dad died after a long progressive illness, no one in his family or himself felt his presence, or dreamed of him. However, one night Steven was visited in a dream by a man who was very calm and bright, a reassuring presence in a uniform standing beside his bed. This man—who Steven later understood was a spirit guide—showed him an image of his dad playing baseball (a sport he had lived for) and Steven woke up knowing that his dad's spirit was okay.

This may sound a bit vague, but this kind of dream interaction is a very common way that people experience spirit contact. The message may be something very simple, but it will be right on the mark when it comes to the person in question. It will be undeniable, and it will bring you peace. This is how it feels when you're visited by your guides.

Trusting Your Intuition

If you read my first book, *A Little Bit of Intuition*, you'll know that when intuition or psychic messages are accurate, they come without fanfare, no huge emotion or anything dramatic. These messages may be so matter-of-fact that you may not recognize them at all. It's not much different with spirit-contact dreams. One client told me that three weeks after her grandmother died, she had a dream that she was sitting at dinner with everyone in her family—including her grandmother—and everyone was fine. She wasn't sure if this was a sign, because the dream was so simple. I find that these are the most authentic dreams of contact. The energy of your departed loved ones is appearing to you in a very straightforward way, and you can see that they are content just a few weeks after passing.

Other people have more classic experiences of spirit contact where the grandpa who just died shows up in their dream and points to something—so, a message of advice or intervention. It might be that Grandpa is pointing to a closet—so go check this closet again for anything you might have missed. Maybe he is pointing to a pet who is still alive. That could be a sign that he misses the dog or cat, or that you need to check something out to help your pet. Some may have a dream of their departed mother showing them a person they don't know. Be open to these messages, because you may meet this person in the future and it could be a warning bell, or your mother could be showing you your future wife or husband! We don't usually recognize messages like this instantly. Just like many dreams, we have to sit with them and live a bit to understand what the meaning is. If you are craving a dream full of meaning and obsessing or can't let it go, that most likely means it is not a message yet—your desire for one is getting in the way a bit.

Still, while many messages are so simple that they can be missed, it's true that while dream symbolism can be helpful and deep, it can also be very cryptic and hard to figure out. Suppose you go to the closet your grandpa showed you and it's empty. Well, now what? This requires some discussion and digging with people who knew him. Maybe there is nothing in there now, but he used to keep something very important in there that confirms to you it's him—maybe his golf clubs, or a box of old letters. Be patient and let it all reveal itself. It's worth it.

Receiving and Interpreting Dream Signs

If you want to try to encourage or be more open to a message from a spirit, there are a few things you can try. Some spirits communicate to us in dreams, some in physical signs that we can see, smell, or touch, and others speak in symbolic coincidences. This exercise can apply to loved ones, spirit guides, or animal spirits.

To Contact a Loved One You Miss

Find a space to sit quietly where you won't be interrupted. Light a white candle if you wish, and burn some sage, incense, palo santo, or whatever herb or scent they may have liked. Take a moment to be sure your heart rate is calm and you are sitting comfortably, ready to meditate. Now bring to mind the person you want a sign from.

If you are reaching out to a departed loved one, I want you to really picture them as though they are right there sitting across from you. It's normal to be emotional doing this, so let your tears out if they come. Keep focusing until you can visualize them sitting across from you. You might remember their voice or their smell, or notice what they are wearing. Take a few moments to feel whatever is coming up and then recenter yourself, calming your heart and breath. Next, I want you to ask them, "Show me what signs you will send to me when it is really you." Trust whatever you hear, feel, or see after this question. Keep picturing them there and keep asking until you are shown a sign, hear something, or smell something. You might see them point to an object, or you may get a mental flash of an object. You might hear a song in your head that meant something to them or to you both. You might suddenly smell flowers, cigars, or rain. The smell will be symbolic for something that means a lot to you or them, and it may just be them telling you they will appear to you as a smell of this flower, or they will appear to you on rainy days somehow.

This is a highly intuitive exercise, so you need to be very open and trust yourself, and this might take some time if you're emotional. Be patient: this will work in time. Your signs from them will start to appear, and there will be a pattern to them. It takes time to see patterns. They have to repeat, so keep a journal of them and you will see over time how this person visits you.

To Contact a Spirit Guide or Animal Spirit

You can repeat the same exercise for loved ones with spirit guides! Here is a slightly different way to connect.

Pick a favorite place you like to go alone. This could be a trail in the woods, a tree in your yard, a path along a river, a fountain in the park. Be sure you are there alone or will be able to remain uninterrupted. Pick a spot to sit down and get comfortable there. Take in your environment for a minute, all the beauty of why you love it here. Imagine that you have light and sunshine surrounding your whole body. Take a moment to really visualize this.

Now ask yourself this: Am I alone? You know logically you are *sitting* here alone. But do you *feel* alone, really? Notice the sounds around you that indicate that you are not all alone—the birds, the crickets, distant traffic, the flow of the water, the sound of the wind. You are never alone, in truth. Now, imagine that there is a presence around you that is very peaceful and comforting to you: a feeling of a companion. Let that sink in. You might feel this as your own higher self—that side of you that is wise and knows what to do, knows the truth of a matter despite your worries and fears. Your higher self is the part of you that knows you have to eat better even though you don't want to. This part of you is always there, but now I want you to listen to it. Who is this wise version of you? Do you feel a different energy than your usual sense of yourself? Does this presence feel like it *is* you? Or does it feel like someone else? If it seems to be different than you, is it male or female? Old or young? Do you know them somehow? Keep bringing in this energy and let the details and sensations come to you.

Trust this process. If it's not coming clearly right away, don't worry. Keep doing it. Most people tell me that as they check in with themselves in this way, gradually they start to feel a sensation of someone there. Sometimes it is them, and sometimes it is a spirit guide. Either way, it's good! You can access your own higher self and develop a relationship to it to help guide you. *If* it's your spirit guide, you will gradually get more information on who this presence is. You might need to go to your sacred spot to feel it at first, but eventually you will be able to feel it around you anywhere. It will be just like any other person you know well; you'll know it's them. This can take time, but persist! Eventually you will be able to ask them for guidance wherever you are.

Always try to write things down, even if they feel strange or unclear at first. Having a record of your experiences will start to reveal the pattern that will allow you to trust the presence of your loved ones or guides.

CHAPTER 4

Tangible Signs

S MELLS, MOVED OBJECTS, FOUND ITEMS, FEELING
a presence, hearing a song: people get all manner of physical
signs that a spirit is trying to communicate or leave a sign. Once you
connect to the way your spirit speaks to you, the "coincidences" will
be uncanny at times. Songs can come on or seem to take over a radio.
Dimes, pennies, or dollar bills can mysteriously appear in places where
you wouldn't expect them. You may smell roses, or the perfume or
tobacco of a lost loved one. You may feel that person standing in the
doorway or near your bed. Your dog might bark at a certain area of a
room, or the cat may sit there staring at it. Your child may also see
something you can't, waving or laughing at what seems like empty
space. People have told me so many things that have happened. It's
very individualized.

One client who came to me pretty regularly for a few years once told
me her grandfather had died, and he was in another country in South
Asia. She couldn't afford to fly there for the funeral and felt awful
about it. She sat there looking quite sad and forlorn and perhaps a bit
guilty. She needed to feel some sort of sign. I suggested that she make
an altar to him in her own home. I told her to place his photo, flowers,

an object or two that belonged to him if she had it, or something that represented him, in a particular spot. After that, I suggested she light a candle every night and pray for him, talk to him. She did this and came back a while later to tell me she had received a sign. I asked her what it was, and she said every day when she set the flowers a certain way on the altar, she would later notice that they had moved. There was no one living with her, no cats to play mischief. His spirit was rearranging the flowers. She felt at peace after that, and that's what's most important.

When I was growing up, I didn't get to meet either of my grandfathers. Both had passed before I was born. At one point, I became intrigued and wanted to know more about my mom's dad because he had a very interesting history, and I wanted to connect to the land where we came from on his side when I went to England in 2019. Sometimes I thought I felt him around, here and there; but, having never met him, I wasn't sure. All I knew was that I felt suddenly compelled to go to England and be there. As I explored more about where he was from, I discovered that the small parish in Cornwall where he was from, and his dad before him, was one of the sites where they shot the *Poldark* television series. The whole family had been watching it at the time, and I had no idea. It almost gave me goosebumps. At the same time, I found out that my brother—who lives across the country from me and hasn't communicated with me much in the last few years—was also thinking of going to the United Kingdom. I had this vibe that perhaps Grandpa was trying to bring the family together from beyond the grave. One night, after I'd returned from my trip where I had stood on the rocky coastal shores where he was born, I was at home and was almost asleep when I saw him standing in my bedroom. His presence was very tangible.

Every time I get messages like this, I verify the details by telling my mom what happened. In this case, I described my grandpa's demeanor, his mannerisms, and the sense of just how serious and severe he seemed. She confirmed that I had described what he had been like in life. So even for me, a professional medium who has been doing this kind of work for many years, his spirit didn't come through so strongly that I was sure beyond a doubt that it was him. Perhaps he wasn't ready, or I wasn't, for a more direct contact; but either way, it led to more discussions with my mom about her life than we'd ever had before. These conversations had a healing effect on me. You may think that a direct contact with someone who has passed on is the most desirable outcome of mediumship, but it can be scary. While that is certainly one way the contact can happen, sometimes a more indirect visitation can lead to positive effects right here on Earth.

I had a regular client many years ago who was trying to sell her home. It was beautiful. The first time she visited me, I had obviously never seen it, but saw it clairvoyantly in my mind: a gorgeous, historic, two-story home hanging in the clouds, trees floating below it. I kept saying it was a mansion in the sky. This image was a bit confusing to me, because it seemed to come right out of a fairy tale, so I thought it must be partly metaphoric. However, my client said, "No, that's exactly right. We even used to call it that!" Her home was a two-story mansion ... at the top of a historic stone apartment complex. It was a gorgeous penthouse overlooking the Montreal mountain, so the floating trees in my mind were accurate. The issue was that she had been trying to sell this house for years—for all I know it still isn't sold. She brought people in to help cleanse it spiritually, real estate agents to assess it, Feng Shui practitioners to rearrange its contents for more energetic alignment. All this is to say she was trying everything—except the advice I gave her. Since the get-go, I'd felt the presence of her father there. He had lived there many years, and he had passed many years before she first came to me. And no matter what she tried, she would come back frustrated, saying it wasn't selling, and I would again tell her, "Your dad's spirit is still in there and he wants you to ask his permission to sell the house so he can leave it and cross over." I respect people's grief process, but it was really hard to watch the years of frustration and financial loss she was enduring because she couldn't quite say goodbye to his spirit yet. He wasn't leaving pennies, or moving objects, but he *was* blocking the sale of a property. I have seen this many times.

For some people it's songs that come on at opportune moments. Many people also tell me about animal or bird messengers as well— this is a common occurrence. In essence, the spirit sends a tangible sign of a bird or stray cat, or a fox that crosses your path, to let you know—*I am here*.

Martha's Cardinal

Martha's dad passed many years ago, and it wasn't an easy relationship, but they had made some peace before he died. She did most of that as inner work and forgiveness of a father who didn't understand how his actions had hurt her. About a month after his passing, she was visited by a beautiful bright red cardinal and instantly felt something around her. It didn't feel like just a bird landing on the fence; it had more of a mystical quality, as if someone or something else was present, or as if it had a message for her. This cardinal landed there every day for a week; and each time, she felt this sensation and each time, she wondered: could this be my dad's spirit? The cardinal lingered and looked at her each time. With this regularity and focus, the cardinal called her away from whatever she was doing to commune with its presence, seemingly recognizing that she was always thinking of her dad whenever it landed. She realized that this was how he was going to speak to her—her sign. There were several times in the years after that her cardinal would arrive at an opportune moment, and she always felt that her dad was around her. Many people say this and experience this with birds. They can be a sort of winged messenger from our loved one's spirit, very comforting. Cardinals in particular are often thought to be visitors from the other side.

Spirit-Guide Signs

Spirit guides show up in a very different way. The relationship you have to a spiritual being is necessarily different, as it is an energy and not a person you knew in a tangible way. Usually guides show up to offer a sign or message. They don't really need to send you objects or songs, but they may suddenly be felt or allow themselves to be seen to indicate something to you. Once, a client of mine was lost while on vacation, walking through a village she didn't recognize, and she didn't know which way to go to find her way back to the right road. She took a deep breath and asked for a sign that would show her which way to start walking. Her spirit guide came into her mind at that moment and pointed. She followed that direction and it led her back to the main road. Your guide may show up in this way to indicate a direction in which to go, whether literal or figurative: which apartment to rent or home to buy, which person to date or not, whether to take a new job or stay at your current job. These interactions themselves are usually quite literal. The guide will show itself to you once you have a relationship and openness to its presence.

Ringing in the Ear

This is another tangible way that spirits can speak with us or give us a sign if they are ready to speak to us. Many people experience a ringing in one ear or increased ringing in the ears before a message is received; or they begin to channel—this allows a free flow of words, sounds, and messages to come to them. If your right ear rings, it's usually a good spirit; the left ear ringing might not always be a spirit who is in the light.

Seeing Light Orbs

This is a really common one, but it is so cool when it happens to you. Lots of people report seeing light orbs floating around a room. These are usually good spirits. I've seen so many myself and heard so many people's accounts of them. One of the most interesting times this happened for me was when I was asked to cleanse the energy of a funeral home. The owners asked me to come a couple of times a year, just to help any lingering spirits cross over to the light. I will never forget the day I first went into the crematorium and there were light orbs floating everywhere! It was almost like a snowy day, the air filled with large slow-moving snowflakes. A peaceful and ethereal feeling hung over the room. So, if you see light orbs, this can also be a sign that someone is around, including a guide, a fairy, a being of light, or another good spirit.

Each spirit has its way of speaking when and if it is ready. There is no right, wrong, or "better" in this kind of communication. It is a language that you simply need to learn if you wish to understand what is being communicated. Dreams are easier than interpreting tangible signs, because we aren't awake to manipulate what we've seen. A dream is a dream. The appearance of a bird can take longer to recognize and interpret. Lost objects that keep reappearing are more obvious to imagine you didn't orchestrate their movements, but songs playing on the radio at particular times may mean something to you that is harder to believe or prove at first. You have to trust your intuition on these matters. You have to make sure you're not walking around craving a sign all the time. They come when you aren't expecting them. You can't force things to be meaningful just because you want a sign. Signs will come when you are gentle with yourself, your energy is grounded, and you know you aren't hanging on to things and making them mean something on demand. It's so beautiful when you let go and see the spirit communications that are happening.

Symbolic Coincidences

Please don't hate me for saying this, but many times we find magical coincidences in things that actually don't add up to much or mean anything at all. For example, say that you keep seeing the number 7: your last apartment number was 7, and then you got a bill today for $7.00 at Starbucks. "Isn't that weird?" you think. Sorry, but—not so much, no.

It is wonderful when we awaken to signs and symbols, because everything feels alive and connected. There is a high that comes from feeling that everything is connected, and a sense of wonder and magic is added our lives. What it means when everything starts to feel coincidental is that you have been awakened to the synchronicity between all things that has always been there! And this is a beautiful chapter for you. But it requires a bit more work! After the stage at which we begin to see synchronicity in our lives, it's important to differentiate the coincidental chaos from the true signs and meaningful symbols—and that's sometimes difficult to do.

Sometimes the repetitive numbers come in a way that *is* a message from Spirit as opposed to our conscious minds. Take Angel Numbers or Master Numbers, for example. When their intuition opens up, many people start seeing Master Numbers all the time, usually on a clock: 1:11 or 2:22, sometimes 3:33. Some people see sequences instead: 12:34, 2:34, etc. How is this phenomenon different from coincidences that don't mean anything, then? Here's the difference: if I am not seeking to find connections and parallels where there aren't any, then I am not in a state of desire or craving. The experience isn't forced.

This is the telltale way of differentiating a real sign or message from something we're desiring or projecting. For most people, the numbers they see show up completely randomly. They aren't trying to stop what they're doing and turn to the time at an exact minute on the clock, but that's what keeps happening. So instead of this being a game of "go figure," it's the identification of a pattern, and the pattern happens to be Master Numbers, which in turn symbolize higher vibrations.

In the case of signs from a loved one or a spiritual being, numbers might be a way they initiate contact. If you happen to notice a pattern of a number or numbers that keep showing up at the same time that you are either feeling or dreaming of someone who has passed, this could be a sign from them. That number will mean something specific for you and that person—maybe it's their old address, their age, a phone number—it's possible. Sometimes the same name keeps popping up as a pattern—you'll see their name on a poster, then an ad, then a business card, then meet someone new with this name all within a very short window of time, like a few days. This can also be a sign if that name means something to you or them—it doesn't have to be their actual name. These types of signs are more closely aligned with mental mediumship: flashing images in your mind, symbolic patterns where others might not see them. My clients often tell me about patterns of tangible signs that ultimately turn out to be a spirit making contact: meaningful songs playing, birds showing up, possessions falling off shelves or dressers.

Anne's Sign of Love

Anne has been single for a number of years and genuinely wants to meet someone but hasn't met the right person yet. Some days it really gets her down. But over these years, she has noticed that spirit guides give her signs on her toughest or loneliest days. One time when feeling very low after a promising relationship didn't work out, she was wondering if she should just give up on love altogether when she was served her bowl of latte. On the top of the foamed milk, there was a big heart. She looked up in glee at the barista, who smiled back. This was a little sign not to give up. Another time, in a similar vein—the idea of giving up pushing into her consciousness—Anne was walking along the sidewalk and noticed a squirrel frantically running in circles around the base of a tree. She stopped to look and noticed an acorn on the ground. The acorn was split in half and was heart-shaped inside. This kind of sign can't be manufactured, can it? And yet it can't be denied. When you are open to living with signs and discern the meaningful ones, life becomes very rich and will give you hope when you need it.

Interpreting Symbolic Messages

I absolutely *love* this part of my work. I have been fascinated with symbolism since my early high school days and adore helping people interpret the signs they get in a dream or other message. There are two things I'd say are important when figuring out what something means. One is to do a bit of research, see if your dream or sign has any classic, historical meanings, and check if it is different in different cultures. You can get a message that is simply a color, and there will be many interpretations based on culture. The second part to remember is that you need to be playful and creative about it—and that's always fun!

Years ago, a friend was going to see a body therapist to help her work through her childhood experiences. During her months of work, she kept saying that her feet were always sore. This therapist said that the feet represent understanding. Quite literally! You stand on your feet, so they are under you as you stand. From there she explored what she was being asked to understand more deeply, and her pain gradually got better. This is a method of interpretation that is both creative *and* backed up by cultural practice and research.

Signs and symbols are rarely just literal. If you are too focused on getting a literal or concrete sign, you will miss the symbolic. At the same time, if you crave signs and start bending every experience into a sign, it's not reliable. You really have to rely on your intuition here, meaning that if a sign or symbol comes to you in some form, and you are compelled or guided to interpret it a certain way at a time when you aren't obsessing in your head or feeling a bit desperate for an answer, then the chances are that this sign is real.

Examples of Symbolic Signs

Trees often speak to us symbolically. If someone passes and their favorite tree is suddenly cut down, or loses its leaves, or suddenly blooms—it is a symbolic sign of their presence. If you dream of your spirit guide for the first time and they are standing beside a big, beautiful tree, you can interpret this in a couple of ways. You can see the tree as shelter: their protection of you. You can see the tree as growth: things they will teach you. You can see what type of tree it is they are standing near, which could be symbolic. Is it an oak, which represents power, courage, and longevity? Or is it a cedar tree, symbolizing healing and cleansing? If it was a birch, it could mean new beginnings. These particular associations are mostly Celtic, but you can find similar meanings for these trees in other cultures. For example, to the Greeks, the oak was said to represent Zeus, the king of the gods—strength, nobility, and protection. To the Norse cultures, the oak represents Thor, the thunder god, and to the Celts it also had associations with fertility and was thought to be the center of wisdom. Any time you have a symbolic message or dream, you can stick to the interpretation that resonates most with you, but it can really widen your understanding to look at a symbol's meaning in multiple cultures. You can interpret signs and symbols on many levels at the same time.

We could take this interpretation one step deeper and see what season or weather it was when your guide appeared by this tree. Was the tree full of leaves, or were some of its leaves starting to fall away? Was the tree healthy or dying? All of this subtle information is usually in your dream, vision, or sign. All of it can turn out to be highly meaningful as a message.

If you get a very symbolic dream or message of a spirit around you, of any nature, first do your research to see what resonates for you most as you read up on it. However, your intuition will be the strongest force for interpretation. This is the strongest and most accurate indicator. So how do you learn to you trust your intuition more?

How Do We Identify
True Intuition?

It's really important to understand what true intuition is, as opposed to our fears, fantasies, projections, and preconceived notions. Learning how to trust intuition in our lives is the key to opening up doors to signs and spirit encounters. So how do you *know*? Intuition comes to us without emotion. You have to be quick—down to the millisecond—when you intuit your first images, words, gut feelings, or vibes about any person, place, or thing that crosses your path. If you see something on the news, you'll immediately get a vibe. Details can be discerned from that vibration, or intuitive information, and become your answer. The second you start wondering "What if?" or second-guessing yourself, thinking, "Maybe it means this or that," you are back in your head, not your gut. You have to learn how to hear that very first sensation that comes to you when you meet someone, when you enter a room, when someone asks a favor or announces an engagement, or when you get a sign from Spirit. These situations may seem disparately linked, but in reality they're no different.

If you walk around craving an answer and you are stuck in your brain, you will endlessly analyze and wonder whether what you're feeling is correct. This is head-breaking and crazy-making, right? Does the process of dissecting your feelings *ever* give you your answers? Rarely. What does give you confidence to proceed is when you get a strong gut feeling and hear a voice that says "yes" or "not now" or "in three months." You can trust the vibe you got when your body has a sudden reaction, like an energy boost or drop at the sight of someone, or upon entering a space.

The same phenomenon applies to messages from spirit guides or loved ones. At first you may get a vibe from the other side, and you will feel that something is a sign, even if you don't know what or who it is. You may not understand it at first, but trust it! Don't worry about what this feeling means right away—just trust that your intuition is telling you that this is a sign. Over time you will see more signs, and patterns will emerge. It might be as simple as thinking, "Hmmm, I'm getting that feeling again. This is a sign. Someone is around me." Gradually, as this happens more, you will notice it is a consistent presence, then can identify it as the energy of someone you've lost, or as a spirit guide who is there around you. You may also notice, as this presence becomes steadier, that certain smells, songs, words, numbers, or signs from nature will appear. This is a process of self-trust and is beautiful when you let it unfold with patience.

If you would like to go further with your intuitive development, I wrote a book on it called *A Little Bit of Intuition*. Take a look if you'd like to get a breakdown of what intuition means, and more examples of it, as well as exercises that will give you a general boost in your confidence to take the leap and trust yourself.

Asking for Signs

If you are ready to open up your world and ask for signs, it is very simple. At the same time, it will be a challenge for you to shift your typical thought patterns. Are you ready?

The best way to begin to get signs is to be very open-ended. Find a quiet spot, or do this in bed when you've just woken up or are just about to fall asleep. Relax your body and breathe deeply until your heart rate is calm. Have your arms open beside you with your palms open and facing up, ready to receive. Gently say to yourself, or out loud, "Universe, show me a sign. Show me what you want me to know." Sometimes you will get an immediate intuitive hit, such as a flash of an image or a word. For most, it will take a bit of time.

After you try this exercise for the first time, you should continue to be mindful throughout your day for the next few days. Pay attention to details, patterns, and synchronicities with more openness than you ever have before. Remain curious and keep observing without any stress and without needing to have an answer or explanation right away. Just observe what happens after this intention is set, and stay open. Write everything down during this process. At some point, you will feel confident that something is a clear and undeniable sign for you.

Classic Signs of Spirits and What They Mean

RINGING IN THE EARS

Usually people hear ringing in their ears when a spirit is trying to speak. Whenever I see people whose abilities are just beginning to open, there is always a period of time where they go through the ringing phase. Just relax when you feel ready and say, "I'm ready to hear you." Take what you hear with a grain of salt just in case, but allow yourself to be open to the gift of clairaudience.

LIGHT ORBS

Light orbs are usually thought to be positive spirits and souls floating around in the atmosphere. If you feel that one of these orbs represents a presence, try to tune in and ask it for a sign or message. Or simply see if you sense this presence as old or young, male or female, this life or a past life, a guide or an ancestor.

FLICKERING LIGHTS OR SWITCHES TURNING ON OR OFF

It is common for mediums and spiritualists to agree that spirits can speak through electricity and electromagnetic fields. Sometimes spirits will turn lights on and off, or they will flicker when there is a presence. I find this is more a sign of a disincarnate soul—a ghost or being that hasn't gone to the light yet. Always tune in and see what presence you feel is there.

SONGS SUDDENLY PLAYING

This one is really cool and surprising when it happens. Sometimes the radio (whether terrestrial or digital, like Spotify or SiriusXM) just starts playing music even when you didn't put anything on. Sometimes the song will be very specific to your loved one, or to your personal memories. Songs can repeat over and over or be playing in multiple places you go. For example, if you suddenly hear a song your dad loved on a radio, then in a movie soundtrack you're watching, then it's playing at McDonald's or Starbucks while you're in line . . . you get the idea. A repeating song that isn't on the top 40 can be a message or sign for sure.

OBJECTS FALLING ON THE FLOOR, BOOKS FALLING OFF SHELVES

This sign is also very movie-like and can amaze you or scare you, depending on how it happens and what the book or object means. This kind of thing happens a lot to people. For example, you are not sure what to do about something you've been worrying about, and suddenly a book flies off the shelf at a bookstore, and it's the answer you were looking for. Or perhaps you place your keys on the counter at the end of your day, and for a week straight they are on the floor by the morning, and there is no cat or child in the house who could've moved them. I know this sounds like pure Hollywood, but these kinds of stories are true. So, if it happens to you, once again tune into who this presence feels like. Pay attention to the book's title and subject matter as a message. Pay attention also to the symbolism of the object that moves. Keys, for example, can be a sign of *key* information, driving, or opening doors—literally and symbolically.

CHANGES IN ROOM TEMPERATURE

This is a definite sign of spirit activity in a place. Most commonly, areas of a room suddenly become cold areas—although, less often, temperatures inexplicably increase. When there is a spirit residing or stuck in a place, part of the room may become cold or breezy. When you pass through it, you might get chills. Most people sense this change, then start to avoid it, so they clutter it up with stuff. But this only makes the phenomenon worse. If you have an area like this in your home, it needs a cleansing. Declutter, clean, and then refer to page 141 in this book to learn about smoke cleansing, smudging, and protection. It doesn't mean the spirit is bad or evil, so don't get too worried; but if it is causing temperature changes, it is stuck and prompting a lower energy in your home.

SOMEONE CALLING YOUR NAME

Clairaudience can also begin with hearing someone calling your name. This one can be a bit tricky to explain. Sometimes you are hearing your own higher self calling your name. Other times, you are hearing a spirit call your name, and this might be a good sign or not—it's impossible to determine unless you sense the quality of this presence in conjunction with other signs. This phenomenon can sometimes be a loved one calling your name—in that case, you'd hear their voice clearly. Other times, you can be hearing your spirit guide. Again, it's impossible to know for sure where the voice is coming from until you take other signs into account.

CLOCKS STOPPING

Clocks often just stop when there is a presence in a home, or when a person dies. It's a very definitive message to have time literally stop and call your attention. This isn't something that always happens, but there have been too many cases to rule it out.

COMPUTERS FREEZING

I've mainly worked online in the past eighteen months, and in this new Zoom era, I have seen some odd things happen. Sometimes computers freeze or go screwy with erratic behavior around certain days, mainly coinciding with high geomagnetic storms and solar flares, or Mercury Retrograde cycles. However, this past period of doing readings online has made me notice that technology flows easily with good energy, and it freezes, stops, delays, or lags with negative energy. When I sense something difficult or dark around someone, invariably the Zoom doesn't work, drops the connection, or freezes. It happens when negative spirits are present, but also when I speak to clients who are wrapped up in toxic situations. In the past, when there were bad vibes around someone for these reasons, they would have traffic delays, miss their exit on their way to see me, and experience all kinds of distractions and mishaps. Many times the person coming felt discouraged, as if something was blocking them from coming to their reading. And there was. I am familiar with this phenomenon, so I knew they might be late, or things would be hectic on their arrival. In their readings, I focused on clearing the negative energy around them and helped them move on from the source of the bad vibes. Now I do the same thing digitally.

TECHNOLOGY ACTING ON ITS OWN

Digital disturbances can extend beyond simple freezing and call-dropping. Sometimes your phone or computer starts downloading things you didn't touch, opening files you didn't open, sending you things you didn't ask for, and these can be spirits using technology to get a message or sign to you.

BUTTERFLIES

There are many ways animals and birds can be signs, and we've mentioned animal totems briefly (and will cover them in more detail in a later section of this book). Butterflies, though, deserve special mention: they are a classic sign of someone's spirit if you see them around you. The ancient Chinese believed souls moved to the spirit world when they saw a butterfly after someone passed. This sign is so beautiful for people when they notice it happening, and it gives so much hope. It's a sign that a loved one is going to the light or passing peacefully. Other times it is a spirit guide or animal totem for transformation, filled with light and grace.

SMELLS

Smells are another classic sign that spirits are around you, especially our loved ones. When a smell is a sign from Spirit, it will be a scent that isn't present in the environment, and usually you will be the only one to smell it. It might be your grandma's perfume, her mints, Grandpa's cologne or pipe, fresh-cut grass, or the sea. Smell is our closest link to memory, and any smell that comes to you from Spirit will likely evoke a memory of a departed one and can start your connection to them. Spirit guides generally don't use smells.

OBJECTS THAT MORPH

Some spirits are strong enough that they can manipulate objects and actually cause them to change shape. You may find that a possession of yours has been inexplicably bent or seemingly crunched under the weight of something, but there is no discernible source. One client told me about a beautiful turquoise ring she had been wearing to help her open her throat chakra in order to speak her truth. On the night after she finally communicated something very important to a person in her life, she discovered that her ring had been bent into an unnatural shape. This might have been Spirit intervening, or the energy of her personal transformation somehow morphed this ring. At the pagan shop where I worked for years, the lattice work on the wall where clients sat during readings warped and fell off. The whole store had this lattice design on the walls, and this was the only spot where it deteriorated and fell off. The point is that energy can shift the material world! Spirit can also use this method to give us a message—again, interpret this sign in conjunction to others you may be receiving.

COINS ON OUR PATH

This is another classic sign from Spirit. So many people say they find a coin on the ground or on another surface and know their loved one has left it for them.

CHAPTER 5

Intention-Setting

S ETTING AN INTENTION BY THINKING DEEPLY
about what you desire is by far the most common way to attempt
connections to Spirit, spreading across cultures, faiths, and traditions.
It is universal and covers a spectrum of practices from chanting to
devotions to manifestation to prayer. You can manifest a dream. You
can pray for a clear sign. You can ask that that sign be something specific. You can spend time sitting with the hope that your loved one is
in the light, or goes to the light in peace, and many times you will feel
a shift as a result of that exercise—a lovely, light, easy, warm feeling
that comes when a soul has crossed into the light. Intention-setting
can help the process of making a connection to Spirit, helping us feel
a link to the next world with an energy shift, sign, or dream.

You can set any intention you wish in whatever way makes sense
to you, but I will share a prayer to Archangel Michael in case you want
to try it. Michael is a patron saint in the Catholic Church because he
appears to people on their death beds to escort them to heaven, especially if they weren't believers in God, and in this way saves their soul.
He is also called upon in Judaism and Islam. He removes anything
evil or negative in, on, and around us, cuts the cords that bind us, and

delivers us from evil forces, seen or unseen. You can use this basic concept and create a prayer asking that Archangel Michael bring your loved one to the light. Once this happens, people usually get the sign or dream they have been seeking.

Saint Michael the Archangel, defend us in battle.
Be our protection against the wickedness and snares
of the devil; May God rebuke him, we humbly pray;
And do thou, O Prince of the Heavenly Host, by the power
of God, thrust into hell Satan and all evil spirits who
wander through the world for the ruin of souls. Amen.

Helping a Loved One
Go to the Light

How do we help someone who has passed to go to the light, and what does that even mean? There are many spiritual realms in most religions, and for mediums it's similar. There are various evolutions of the soul. Some souls are very much here focused on the earthly plane—they're mostly preoccupied with tangible, practical things like their physical body, their money, or their property; and it's all about what can be seen with our own eyes. Other souls are here to deal with the mental or abstract realm—always tangled up in their thoughts, dealing with communication and deep thinking, possibly grappling with learning issues, or even imbalances of the mind in many forms. They are here to master that realm. Other souls are more concerned with the emotional realm—empathy, identifying and processing emotion, absorbing others' energies as opposed to expressing their own deeper emotions, creativity, and self-expression. There are many levels we can define, and we can be here to do more than one thing, of course; but I wanted to give a progression of sorts, because our soul also has a progression.

When someone passes, there is obvious trauma to the body or physical realm, and some souls take longer to accept or let go of their physical incarnation than others. They might be very attached to places or objects, possessive of people they loved, and generally not ready to fully let go of their earthly life. These souls can be called earthbound. Some souls stay earthbound and get stuck—and others just need some time to transition. This is what I often see when people are not getting any messages from the other side yet. We can help an earthbound soul go to the light, meaning that we can encourage them to accept their passing, the end of their life, and to let go and experience peace in heavenly or cosmic light.

Other souls who were here on Earth working out energetic, mental, or sometimes emotional realms can find it faster or easier to let go of this earthly plane of existence, and so they go to the light faster. Some go instantly! Everyone is different. So, if you have not had a sign or message from a loved one, it could be helpful to do this exercise to gently help them go to the light.

How to Help Someone Go to the Light

1. Find a good spot where you feel comfortable or that means something to you.

2. Pick a good day when you can be relaxed and uninterrupted.

3. If you like, you can light a candle or incense, or burn herbs to sanctify and clear the space.

4. Sit quietly for a few minutes and focus on relaxing your own body and calming your heart rate.

5. When you feel centered and relaxed, visualize a column of light coming down from above that is brighter and clearer than anything you've ever witnessed. Imagine this light surrounding you head to toe, front and back. See this light also entering the Earth below you and send it to the Earth's core.

6. As above, so below. You are protected in Divine Light.

7. Call in your spirit guidance, even if you don't know who they are yet. They will still be there to help this process.

8. Call in the spirit guides of the person you wish to help cross to the light. Just trust that they are there.

9. Gently say the name of who you are helping and say it out loud, or write it on something if you wish, but bring their presence to you.

10. When you get a clear image or sense this person's energy, you can say whatever you wish to them. It's not a goodbye, but it can help you to say things you've been wanting to say.

11. Say their name and give them permission to go to the light. "_____, I grant you permission to go to the light if and when you are ready." See what you feel or sense next. Sometimes you will get a message or a rush of energy, sometimes a powerful feeling of love or fear for a split second.

12. If you see a beautiful light appear around this person or they seem to disappear in a flash of light, you have succeeded. If you see them looking at you with love and joy in your mind, you have succeeded. If you suddenly receive a download of information from them, you have also succeeded. They can still come to you and communicate with you, but now it will be much lighter, clearer, and more joyful.

13. If you sense fear or resistance, or heavy emotions like anger or bitterness, they may not be ready. You can try visualizing the light again and reassure them that their loved ones and guides are there, waiting to help them. Sometimes they will communicate something to you first before they are ready. This could be an instant thing, or it may take a few tries. Don't be discouraged by this process. Keep visualizing and affirming permission to let go and be in the light with their guides and loved ones, and gradually it will happen. When it does, you will know by the signs mentioned in the previous point.

If you want to try this process using Archangel Michael as a guide, I find it very powerful, but you can use any guides you feel best with. Archangel Michael is a saint, but is mainly a spiritual entity that anyone can reach out to no matter what your religion, if you feel comfortable doing so. If not, you can go to any similar spiritual entity who banishes the dark forces and protects with light.

Calling on Archangel Michael: My Version

Say his name three times.

"Archangel Michael, please remove anything in, on, or around us that is no longer for our highest good. Please take your sword of light and cut away any negative bonds, energetic cords, or thought forms that no longer serve us. Surround us in your light, guide us, and help us to ascend from the Earthly plane to Divine Light. Amen."

CHAPTER 6

Meditation

MEDIUMSHIP ISN'T THE GOAL OF MEDITATION, but it can happen that you encounter a spirit while deeply meditating. In 2002, I went to my first Vipassana meditation retreat. This is a very intense form of meditation, because you sit in silence for ten days. You aren't allowed Advil or even a journal. You are there to deal with whatever raw sensation and emotion needs to come up, and to learn to practice the technique during the waves of memory and emotion that will occur. Vipassana teachers don't want to talk, or even allow people who practice Reiki to participate in the training— that's the kind of intensity they are asking practitioners to reach for. I understand why, because this depth of meditation is a gateway for altered states of consciousness, even though the connection between meditation and mediumship isn't often discussed or taught—and in this case was not talked about at all. Still, that doesn't preclude people from entering an altered state of consciousness, as I found out.

Men and women sat on opposite sides of the meditation hall, and usually I was parallel to one certain man on the other side, so we sat many hours and days across from each other. Even though we never spoke or smiled, our energies were aligned. Most of my focus was just on learning and practicing the Vipassana technique and dealing with my own issues, but there were beautiful and blissful moments and sensations too, where I began to channel without trying. I sensed many things about the man across from me and his life; and at the end of the ten days, when we could socialize a bit, I asked him if I could reflect this to him. I was not surprised when my impressions turned out to be accurate. I told the man I felt a baby's soul coming into the lives of him and his partner, and he confirmed that his wife back at home was pregnant. When I received these images, I was in a deep state of meditation—also known as a trance—that opens us up to spirit communication and channeling.

If you want to try opening up to spirit communication during meditation and haven't had any previous experience, I will caution you to do it with a guide at first. You never know what manner of spirit you may encounter, and to be honest it can sometimes be overwhelming or scary. It can also be beautiful and peaceful, but you don't have control over what will come through if you are a beginner. If you do this with an experienced medium who you trust, that person can verify, affirm, and protect you so you have a good experience.

With a regular practice of meditation and a desire to open up to this dimension of life, over time you will most likely feel the spirits of many who are around you, be they ancestors, angels, or spirit guides, animal totems or interdimensional beings. Meditation practice is a very good way to approach this work in general, if you go into it with the meditation technique, not mediumship, as the goal. The ritual of meditating regularly will keep you centered and more present, and therefore able to receive your own sensations. Therefore, your discernment and ability to handle your emotions and insights will improve. When you meditate regularly and develop these abilities, you can trust your spirit-contact experiences much more.

At first, meditation will help you connect to yourself. The myth is that meditation will bring you to a state of bliss, which just isn't true, at least at first. Deep contemplation during meditation is a gorgeous feeling, but it can be fleeting, just like clouds that pass overhead. I find that the mental clarity we reach for during meditation practice tends to happen when we are completely present and have released old energy or trauma, so we have to work through that first to get to the bliss.

What meditation does is help you witness what's going on deep inside you, so at first you will not feel bliss on the cushion—you will feel very emotional or restless, achy or grumpy. At Vipassana, the guru taught that it takes three days of silence to calm the mind. I had breakthroughs on my third and fourth days—they weren't pleasant, but they were a truth I was avoiding. Once I allowed that to dissolve and I cried it out, I was much more honest about my own limitations and started to respect myself on a deeper level, and that is when the lighter, more blissful states began reaching me more; the metaphysical and channeling side of it happened more; and I went deeper than I'd ever experienced as well. So even though I'd already begun my spiritual and self-healing path ten years beforehand, I still had mental and emotional blocks to overcome at this retreat. It was a very healing experience, and I am so grateful to have had them, even though dissembling these obstacles was initially painful. I'm saying this because I want to give you a very realistic sense of what to expect from going deeper into your meditation. If you already have strong abilities to channel, you may not need to sit for very long before the door of your perception opens; but for many people there is a lot of emotional inner work to contend with before channeling or mediumship can be experienced in this way. All is possible, though, and in my opinion everyone benefits from meditation: whether you gain self-awareness and presence, or have a metaphysical experience, it's worth it.

If you want to try meditation to connect with your loved one on your own without a practice or retreat, you can try, and just be patient with it. If you give yourself enough time to sit and truly calm your body and breath, at that point you can pray or speak in your mind to your loved one. It will help you get in touch with your grief and help you release the emotions surrounding it. You can ask their spirit to please come through and give you a sign, in any form. In this case, your meditation is to help you heal yourself and to pray and open yourself up for signs. And they will come.

Meditation to Connect to a Spirit

As I described previously, when you are deep in a meditation for mindfulness, Vipassana, breathwork, or some other practice, it's not uncommon to experience a spontaneous image or feeling of a spirit around you. However, if that isn't happening yet, here is another meditation you can try:

Find your favorite quiet spot and make yourself comfortable.

Start to be aware of your breath. You might feel it in your nostrils or feel the warm or cool air on your upper lip. Take the time to really be still and breathe, relaxing your body inch by inch. When you're feeling deeply relaxed, I want you to picture yourself approaching a bench. It's solid and comfortable and has a view that makes you feel totally safe. Perhaps you overlook a park, a forest, or the sea. Place yourself on this bench and get comfortable there. Imagine your surroundings by looking gently to the left, then to the right. Feel that you are really here in this beautiful spot. Now I want you to see something approaching this bench, walking toward you. Take a moment to really see them and feel them as they arrive. What mood are they in? What are they wearing? Do they look young or old? See whatever you observe.

Next, see them sitting down beside you. Allow yourself to have a conversation with them. Talk to them in your mind. Be open to whatever shows up and try to find out more about them. Trust your intuition with the indications you get from them. When you're this relaxed and the visual comes easily, and you can see or hear responses from them, trust that this is a true visitation.

CHAPTER 7

Channeling

WHEN YOU HEAR THE WORD *CHANNELING*, WHAT
does it bring up for you? Does it seem woo-woo and weird? Or
maybe scary? Or confusing? We usually think of the extremes when it
comes to this word—someone whose body or mind is "taken over" by
a spirit in order to speak. There are many famous mediums who did
this and do it still, but most seem to be in conversation with an entity
or guide. A current one is Lee Harris, an English intuitive who speaks
to his guides, who he calls the Z's. There's Esther Hicks, who channels
Abraham. An older example would be the American medium Jane
Roberts, who channeled a being called Seth and wrote several books
on the wisdom he passed on to her. Not everyone is here to channel to
that level. It's a very demanding process and one that will make your
personal life much harder, since people will be in awe or in fear of your
experience. However, channeling can also be much lighter when we are
not taken over, but more in conversation with a spirit. And in truth, it
can be even lighter than that—channeling can also be inspiration or
motivation by a spirit we encounter, even just someone we like whose
energy we take on. I'll bet you do it on some level already when it comes
to this last form of it.

Think of someone in the motivational speaking world, for example Tony Robbins. He could be said to be channeling something through him when he speaks. Where does this high energy and clarity come from? Is it *all* really coming from him as an individual with a certain experience? This is not to negate his magnetic personality, but to recognize that he is able to tap into a source of energy that is very powerful and translate his message to such a degree that he can make stadiums of people energized and inflame the spirits of millions of followers through his collection of books and programs. When his followers like his program or his methods, they are in essence trying to channel their energy to tap in to what he's got going on so they can benefit from it too. This is still a very light form of channeling. It's not coming from inside you, is it? You're connecting an outside source of energy to your own.

Mediumship is channeling another's energy to the max. Mediums are able to handle allowing their own personality and boundaries to relax in order to allow that other energy into theirs, so to speak.

Although the "taking over the body of" kind of mediumship is a real thing, it is a small part of what channeling can be. This level of engagement can be scary and harmful, so it's not necessarily something you want to aspire to. Some mediums do it and come back out of trance, recover, and are fine, with memories of all that has passed through them. Many will be so deep in trance that they need someone there to record or take notes of what they said, because they weren't conscious enough to commit these lessons to memory. This is a true channel, and it is certainly not for everyone to develop. It can be a very dangerous practice if the person is not psychologically and emotionally ready to handle it.

We all have our inherent capacity for self-awareness. We all have the ability to feel other people's vibes or energies. Whether we feel comfortable or capable enough to allow those energies to affect us, enter us, motivate us, or even speak through us is unique to every individual.

Automatic Writing

One of the best ways to begin to channel in general is to do automatic writing. What is this, and how does it work? Think of a time you were telling a story at a gathering and getting into it. Everyone was listening and enjoying it as you spoke, and you found yourself saying something really funny or clever that you didn't plan: it just came out. Where did this come from? If it was a manner of speaking that you don't often use, then how did those brilliant lines just come out of your mouth? Usually, people will joke with us in that moment and say that our sudden virtuoso performance came out of the depth or poetry of our expression. Did you hear those words in your mind and were in such an intuitive flow that you just said them without censoring yourself? Likely, yes. Another possibility is that you were channeling. You may have been hearing your higher self—that part of us that we don't often access but holds our deeper wisdom. Perhaps you heard those words from a spirit guide around you. If you start practicing automatic writing, it is a great way to get in touch with this energy and begin to channel.

Automatic Writing Exercise

Grab a good pen and lots of paper, and get settled.

Light a candle.

Put yourself into a calm meditative state. Maintain good posture. Make sure you're physically comfortable and that you have privacy, no distractions, and that you calm your breathing for a few moments until you really feel your heart rate slow down and get a sensation of stillness or "going within."

Take your pen and paper and begin to gaze at the candle flame.

You will not be looking at what you write.

Keep gazing at the candle until words and thoughts come to mind clearly enough so that you can write them down.

Be patient and write down every thought that comes to you—they will be random and nonlinear and make no sense at first. Keep writing it all. Alternately, you can keep the pen moving no matter what comes. This will create a stream of consciousness on the page. You might end up writing something like dog, ball, food, tomorrow, run in the park, six years old, our dog was called Sparky, my pants are ripped. . . . You get the idea.

It can seem very random or awkward at first to pay attention to all the thoughts that run through your brain and record them. However, you will start to have insights that come in the middle of this stream. Sometimes the next line after "my pants are ripped" is "the nature of reality is such that letting go IS love," then it goes back to "I want pizza." We allow the stream and flow to begin, and it will be all over the place with flashes of insight.

As you continue to write, your guides and spirits will also come and speak through you. You might be on the third page of automatic writing when you suddenly hear the voice of an old soul whispering a word or two, saying your name, or you may hear a phrase from your great-aunt who passed a couple of years ago. You can't control it at all. When you channel, you become a vessel. A vessel receives and doesn't demand, ask, or dictate. This exercise is one of the best ways to open yourself up to hear this flow and begin to channel.

CHAPTER 8

Intuition

WE TOUCHED ON INTUITION ALREADY IN THE context of discerning signs from Spirit, but it deserves a little more attention for its use as a tool for spirit communication. Intuition is a light form of channeling. You have intuition whether you are aware of it or not. You pick up information from people, places, environments, energetic dynamics, objects, art, music, and on and on. In most situations, without even thinking about it, you'll feel the vibes in the environment around you and download what's happening very quickly. You'll usually make a choice on autopilot based on your gut reaction. It is when you make the intuitive information you've derived part of conscious thought that you begin to open the gateways to channeling.

If you walk past a few restaurants looking for the best place to eat, you may base your decision on a feeling you are getting. In the kinds of situations where you just go with your gut, you aren't studying the menu, the history of the business or the building, or interviewing the guy on the patio sitting there enjoying a meal. Instead, you are processing intuitive information so fast, you don't even know it. You base your choice on the energy you receive.

You do the same thing when you walk into a home or apartment you are thinking of renting or buying. You may have done a bit more research beforehand, but you are still basing your ultimate decision at least partially on the vibe you get from the space. It could be perfect on paper—the right location and price, with new appliances in working order—but perhaps you feel a sadness in it, or sense something odd from a neighbor or even the building itself. You have no proof, but this feeling becomes a factor in your decision-making process, and though it is not based on logic, this kind of assessment is generally accepted as a good reason to pass on or pursue a place to live. Channeling based on intuition is the practice of developing this gut feeling and learning to trust it to gain information about the world.

Everyone in my intuition trainings is always amazed at how strengthening our intuitive power awakens them to trust themselves more and more, be specific about what they sense, and go with it. Intuition is a power that increases over time. The more you use it, the higher the level of detail and flow of energy you can sense. Sometimes that energy you sense will be spirits. Check out the exercise that follows for an initial intuition-strengthening practice. And, if you want even more information, refer to my first book, *A Little Bit of Intuition*. We can all increase our abilities in this life and create more meaning and flow to help us.

Connecting with Intuition

An amazing way to connect to your loved ones with your intuition is psychometry. Psychometry is the practice of taking an object and reading its vibrations. I often ask clients for an object owned by the person they wish to connect with, and tell them to hold it while I channel to connect to their vibration. It's very powerful and easy for you to do, too. If you have a piece of your loved one's jewelry, a watch, keys, a shirt or a scarf, or something they always had on a shelf like a figurine or a framed photo, you can use it to connect to them.

Psychometry to Connect to Loved Ones

Center yourself and get quiet somewhere comfortable.

Place the object between your hands.

Close your eyes and focus on the feelings you get. Does the object feel warm? Do you feel sensations in your hands or elsewhere in your body as you hold it?

Allow any imagery to come to mind, and go with it. They might be trying to show you something, and you will see a flash image of something. It might not make sense to you right away, and you might need to ask someone who knew them if the image makes sense literally or as a metaphor.

Allow any words or phrases to come to mind. You might hear the person with whom you are trying to connect speaking in your mind. Allow it to come and don't doubt things—just keep going with it and write down what you've heard afterward so you can review it all later. Eventually, as your mediumship abilities open, you may feel your loved one speaking to you directly.

Pay attention to any other level of sensation that arises, since that could be a message—sudden songs in your head, smells that are not in the room, or strong memories that come back to you.

Connecting to Spirit Guides with Intuition

This is another great writing exercise that can help you connect to your guides. It is taken from classic inner-child work. You'll need some paper and a pencil, pen, or crayons.

First, fold the paper in half. Your dominant hand writes a question, and your non-dominant hand answers the question. When doing inner-child work, participants start by asking, "What does my inner child wish to say to me?" Then, they try to relax and see what their non-dominant hand is compelled to write. To connect with guides, start by asking something like, "I would like to speak with my spirit guides. Are you present?" See if you hear a yes or no. Write the answer with your non-dominant hand.

If you get a yes, you can ask some general follow-up question like, "Are you male or female?" "Have I known you before?" "How old are you?" "How long have you been with me?" It's best to build a rapport and get used to the dynamic of allowing the answers to flow from your intuition before you start asking about your current problems or the mysteries of life. The very process of doing this exercise opens up your intuition and, over time, can help you connect to your guides more profoundly.

Part 3

All Manner
of Spirits

MEDIUMSHIP IS ANY COMMUNICA-tion to a spirit or entity—so this includes many forms of energy, including ancestors, spirit guides, angels and saints, gods and deities, animal totems, pet spirits, interdimensional beings, entities, and disincarnates. You can experience contact and communication with any of these, so discerning which is which can be a long journey. The next section will detail some of the various spirits you can encounter, including the best methods for doing so and what you can expect from them, positive or negative. Allow me to help you navigate this next step of spirit communication and make it a positive experience!

CHAPTER 9

Ancestors

W HEN YOU CONNECT TO ANCESTORS, THIS
includes the loved ones you knew in this life who have
passed, but it also includes anyone in your family lineage going back
centuries in time. It's often hard to verify some of the information that
comes through about a great-grandfather you never knew and about
whom you most likely don't have verifiable or even anecdotal information. Very often, when a person's ancestors come through, they will
mention places and people they are with that you don't know anything
about. Your great-great-grandmother might be telling you she loved a
favorite house and will show it to you clairvoyantly, but you have never
seen her nor the house, and no one in the living world may have seen
or heard about it either. What then?

People often shut down these messages when they can't instantly
verify them. However, it would help you to fully listen to what your
ancestors say before asking yourself whether or not the source is real
and the message is true. Why? Because there is always a reason they
show you what they do. There is always a message in it somehow, even
if it initially seems opaque—it might be a connection to something
that is relevant for you or your parent on that side of the family. This

communication might also simply be a real-life, mundane way for you to get a feel for your ancestors' lives so that you feel connected to them. Sometimes the locations they show you are relevant to your family history in some way. She may not have lived in the house she is showing you, but it might be a special place to her for another reason—maybe her first love lived there. You have to be totally open to exploration so this type of message can come through.

When it comes to the spirits of the departed, many people will recognize who a person is by physical appearance and a few details of their basic character, whether from personal experience or from anecdotes related by other family who knew them. This information is helpful when it comes to identifying that a spirit is definitely an ancestor, which can help you stay open to what other messages are coming. Sometimes the spirits of your loved ones' friends who knew them in life will also show up to give you insight about them. Your mom's best friend growing up, your uncle's business partner he knew for thirty years—you may not immediately know these people, but they may have things to tell you as well. Stay wide open during a session so you can benefit from the amazing ways messages come through.

Say that you did know your grandparents, but when they come through, they show you something you can't fully verify, like their favorite shirt or another mundane object from their life that you wouldn't normally recognize. Remember, there is a reason for this message, even though it may seem confusing. Maybe that shirt was worn on the day your parent was conceived or was what they were wearing the day World War I broke out—some turning point that was significant in their lives and the life of your family. How does that make sense as a connection to your life now? Perhaps everything changed for your family on the day that shirt was worn, and the aftereffects are still there emotionally in your family dynamic. Messages come through as clues that will lead to healing. Staying open and curious is key. You can figure out what their communications might mean upon reflection after your session is done.

It has always surprised me how many people will block this kind of contact during a reading, even though it is so rich with healing insight. People will look baffled and say, "But I never knew my aunt," and I will say, "Okay, but she is here and was your mother's sister, so perhaps she has insight into your mom or you as a child. Do you want to ask anything?" Most of the time, people will just shrug and say no. But if, similarly, you reject this kind of contact, just remember that you're missing out on some beautiful potential to learn more about certain aspects of yourself, your childhood, your mother's life, her experience with you. . . . It makes me sad when people do not stay open to *all* ancestors who show up versus the single person they are grieving at present.

Maybe the ancestor showing up was the family black sheep and has messages that would help you understand deep family patterns and trauma. Maybe they will share something about your early childhood that explains why you have a hard time with something currently. It's worth your while to be completely open and receptive to whatever and whoever comes through during your reading with a medium.

CHAPTER 10

Spirit Guides

I LOVE SPIRIT-GUIDE CONNECTIONS. THAT MAY BE because I have a spirit guide myself: I am always connecting to a light being that speaks clearly, positively, and with high energy, and I get a lot of comfort and encouragement from this contact. Most people aren't aware of who their spirit guides are. Neither was I for a long time. I wanted to make sure I wasn't making up a fantasy character who I *wished* was around me, so instead I took years to observe the strong experiences that came through, until I was satisfied that it was really happening.

A spirit guide relationship is unlike any other. In order to know a new person in your life, you need time, intimacy, and observation of their patterns of speech, movement, and more to feel connected. It's no different with a spirit guide. Over time, you can recognize the distinct energy and pattern of this guide and be sure it is them when you make contact. Once that connection is strong enough, you'd recognize them anywhere right away, just like we would all know our mother or father anywhere. Until you've developed your connection to this level of certainty, you should be wary of taking any messages too seriously. Be open to the guidance that comes through in a reading, but do take it all with a grain of salt and observe whether the information your guide imparts turns out to be relevant and helpful for you.

Spirit guides never use negative language. They don't tell you what to do and won't give directions or advice in a "you should" tone. True spirit guides will indicate things in a gentle and very simple way. They don't speak in long complex sentences. Many times, if you are working with a medium, she might translate a spirit guide's communications into symbolic terms so that you understand the message. For example, if you come to me and request that I connect you to your guides so you can ask them if you are on the right track with your career, I may be shown a curving road with a cliff beside it as an image. I may see your guide standing on a certain part of the curve and smiling. This is the way guides often speak to us—through images and symbols. This leaves us with two choices as mediums—we can literally tell you about that image and leave you to figure it out, or we can interpret it for you and try to impart advice based on the metaphor and the vibe of the message. In this example, I would say there are many changes ahead, and some could feel risky or scary—the cliffs and the curving road. However, because the guide is standing at the curve and smiling, that could mean that you will be guided when you get to this turning point or big decision or risk. It could also be that the smile says, "Don't worry, you will make the right choice and be safe." The smile could also be showing me that this next series of twists and turns is all good, all part of your growth path. People get super-frustrated with this kind of communication in readings. They want us and their guides to say, "Apply for that job you saw on LinkedIn last Tuesday at 2 pm—that's the right job and it'll all be perfect." So sorry, but it doesn't work that way. You asked, "Am I on the right path with my career?" and your guide may be showing you the path and some of its features, but you're out of luck if you go in expecting directives and guarantees.

My Spirit Guide

I won't reveal exactly who my spirit guide is, because for me it's very personal and sacred, but I do want to share the important parts of how I came to recognize and build the trust in him. It was 2001, and I had just broken up with a long-term boyfriend, changed my career, and moved to a new neighborhood, and I was all alone for the first time after a few intense years. I was living near a park filled with spiritual activity and having a lot of intense new experiences because of that connection. I was also doing a lot of meditation and automatic writing. I felt compelled to cleanse and restore myself after this relationship and the loss of a dream.

I used to sit and light a candle and allow words to come to me, then write them down. I was in a deeper and more receptive state than I'd been in years. In that chapter of my life, I used to wake up regularly and see a spirit at the foot of my bed. It was always the same—a First Nations man, a chief in a white feather headdress. He didn't say anything. He was just standing at the end of my bed, looking strong and regal. I always felt enormous protection and comfort from him. This went on for a couple of years, or even more. I never tried to summon him—ever. I only observed what happened and how I felt when he did show up.

After that chapter, a new one began where I started to hear a word or name in my meditations, or just randomly as I drifted off to sleep. I could never make out the exact wording, because it was another language. I had a feeling it could be Mohawk, since the figure in my visions was an Indigenous guide and I live on their territory, but I couldn't be sure. I asked a friend of mine, Eric, who is Metis—part Mohawk and part Quebecois—if the name I had heard sounded Mohawk to him, by attempting to recreate the tone of the sounds that were coming through. Just to be clear, I wasn't hearing a full clear name yet, I was getting partials and sounds, as if he were speaking sentences to me in another language. I was trying to describe the rhythms, the staccato, the vowel combos I got, to see if it sounded like Mohawk. Eric wasn't sure enough to confirm. I also asked a friend and fellow student from my Concordia University days, whose mission was helping the Mohawk reclaim their language. He also found it hard to verify at the time. The language and names just weren't clear enough yet for me to verify. That was in 2005. I just accepted this and allowed further communication to unfold.

Flash forward to 2013: I went to Sedona, Arizona for the first time. It was a profound healing experience for me. Words and names were coming to me a bit more often over those eight years, but they were still not clear enough to verify. Still, I stuck with it, wanting to know their source. Sedona was healing, because I met mediums and healers by chance; and many of them told me similar things about myself, which was significant since it reinforced the notion that their opinions were objective, as I heard them repeated again and again.

I met one healer while on my bucket-list trip to the Grand Canyon, flying on a small Cessna plane followed by a helicopter, which flew down to the Colorado River. After we landed, my group got into a boat on the river, flew back up to the Grand Canyon to have lunch, and then flew home. It was pure magic for me. At one point during the trip, I was coming down the rocks next to the river and I felt an energetic line connect from one woman on the plane to me. She called to me out of nowhere and asked, "Are you okay, hon? Need help on the steps?" I was a bit surprised that she suddenly connected to me so strongly. I called down, "Yep! I'm okay, thank you!" We started to chat a bit in the boat, just light and friendly banter. Later, when we'd had lunch at the

Canyon and were getting back on the bus to the plane, she turned and asked, "How do you feel about psychic abilities?" And I turned to her like a crow on a wire and said, "I've been a medium for twenty years." She turned back just as fast and said, "I've been a medium for *thirty* years. You have an entity attached to you right there," and pointed to my back—exactly where I have had pain for years. Right away, she gave me the name of a healer to go see in Sedona.

As I waited a few days to get in to see the healer, I consulted another person, seeking information but providing him with none about myself. Unprompted, he mentioned my past lives as a First Nations woman, who had a very loving family, the daughter of a chief. He also said I needed to learn Reiki or some other modality to learn how to allow the energy to come through me, as opposed to one that would require me to use my own life force. He said I was currently using my life force to moderate the energy of my spirit guide, which was why I was so drained. Allowing energy to come through us—realizing that control—is channeling, whether the energy in question is a spirit or more generalized. In order to prevent the exhaustion and pain I had been feeling, I knew that I needed to learn to trust and allow it to move through me without trying to control it. He also pointed to a spot on my back (the same one that my new friend on the Grand Canyon trip had highlighted!) and said there was an entity attached to me. I said nothing. I now had double confirmation.

A couple of days later, I went to the healer the friend had recommended. She had my number in thirty seconds flat. She looked at the gemstone configuration she'd laid down for me and right away asked me the million-dollar question, the main issue of my life's healing— how did I feel about my dad? I spat out the truth in a single sentence. That's what truth is like. It is simple and straight, without frills, but it also comes with ease and compassion. After we discussed the difficult dynamics of that relationship, she began to clear me of negative energies, including the attachment I still had to my ex—yes, from fourteen years before! Sedona was a huge spiritual cleansing for me and set the stage for what happened next.

When I got home from Sedona, back in my apartment facing the mountain in Montreal—all woodsy, quiet, and sunny—I was able to meditate and receive even more high energy than ever before. When my spirit guide whispered to me as I was going to sleep or in a deep state of meditation, I finally heard not one name but two. I was able to confirm later that both are Mohawk language names, and that they are connected to each other. The spirits of these guides have a history of being healers, and they even have a link to my current home, as well as to where I grew up—a nine-hour drive away. Their names came through so specifically and clearly that I could research them. I was floored, emotional, and very grateful.

I began to look for a good Reiki teacher and started to learn how to allow energy to move through myself and prevent it from draining me as I worked. That was a life-changer that made my life much better.

In case Reiki is something new to you, let me describe it. Reiki as we know it now was founded in the 1920s in Japan by Makao Usui, a Japanese scholar born in 1865. He is said to have received the symbols that comprise Reiki intuitively. These symbols function like a code that can open a certain flow of healing energy. He found that people could help heal each other with it, and help heal themselves as well. It's sort of like when you buy a specialized lamp, and it needs a plug and bulb that are different than the mainstream versions. You plug it in, and it works just like a normal lamp as long as you use its special plug and socket. The Reiki symbols are like that unique plug, and when you are initiated and open the symbols given, it plugs the lamp into the wall, and now we can use that light for healing.

Without fail, and without bidding, every time I open my Reiki symbols, my guide is always just standing there. As I got to know him, he also started showing up more regularly in my readings. He often stands behind the person I'm reading, but in a respectful way—always allowing space, never hovering over anyone's shoulder. He only indicates, points, nods yes or no, or makes simple gestures while the person is talking to let me know what they are sharing.

When my guide shows up, he gives me clear assistance. I do not ask him to come every time, nor do I crave his presence. He will show up if it is meant to happen, and he does so more often than not. He started showing up in my Reiki sessions at first, just to be present. Over the years, he has showed me so much about healing. And at this point my main messages from him during sessions are that he will do the clearing work needed if I just maintain my own light and presence for the person as a vehicle while the session is happening.

I have learned so much from the experience of connecting with my guide. It took years to build this relationship and trust it. We can't just pull meaningful relationships out of thin air; but with an open mind, you can find guides who can help affirm what is happening to you. If you work with an experienced medium like me, we can also help by describing your guides or their messages for you so that you can begin to build the relationship for yourself. It requires patience, but it is definitely worth it. In times of anxiety, I find that my guide is there, and his presence helps me calm down or lets me know what's going to happen. It has been an amazing journey, and I encourage you to take the steps for yourself and begin to build that relationship.

Guided Meditation to Connect to Three Spirit Guides

This next guided meditation is one that I've given to classes many times. My students always experience much rich detail in the messages that come through. You might want to record yourself reading the words below so you can guide yourself through this meditation with your eyes closed. If you are listening to an audio version of this book, you don't even need to do that! And if you have no way of listening to the following meditation, it's still very effective to visualize it as you read it. This practice will connect you to three different types of spirit guides.

You will want to be very relaxed for this exercise so you can visualize well.

Find a comfortable place and position in which to sit so you'll be at ease for twenty to thirty minutes.

Take a few deep breaths and release any tension in your body.

I want you to imagine you're walking along a dirt pathway. Look down and see your feet walking on this path. Notice anything on the ground as you walk. Now look to your left. What do you see? Look to your right and notice your surroundings in detail. Take another deep breath.

Continue walking this beautiful path, and as you walk you'll notice there is a forest up ahead. Keep walking until you reach the path into the woods. Notice all your surroundings once again, looking to the left and to the right. As you walk along, you're feeling wonderful and have a sense of anticipation at what you might discover on your way. You notice there is a large boulder up ahead on the right.

You walk up to this boulder and notice there is an animal on top of it. What animal do you see? Trust your first intuition. What demeanor or mood does this animal have? What body language? Now, ask this animal to show you something you need to know right now. Trust whatever comes to you, be it an image, a word, or a short movie-like sequence. Absorb what this animal is telling you and give thanks to it. You feel filled with new wisdom and continue walking on the forest path.

The forest is getting a bit deeper. You are fully surrounded by the woods and their atmosphere, the temperature of the air, the natural sounds—being in nature is filling you with joy. You feel contentment. As you walk, notice that there is a pond up ahead on the left. Go to this pond and look into the water. What do you notice about this beautiful pond? Look around it everywhere and note any details of your surroundings. As you look a second time into the pond water, you see the face of an ancestor looking back at you. Trust the first vision of the person you see. Take a moment to see them in detail, if you can. You may not know who this is, but you'll figure it out later. Next, ask them if there is anything they want you to know right now. Be very open to any flash of insight that comes to you. Allow yourself a minute, or a few minutes, to receive what is coming through. Take a moment to absorb this and then thank them for their help and presence.

Step away from the pond, knowing that you can come back here any time you wish. Return to the path in the woods. It appears to be growing a bit wider as you go deeper into the forest. There is a clearing of light up ahead, and you feel great anticipation to arrive in this spot. Something feels sacred and magical about it. Continue walking until you have reached the clearing. You have arrived and it is so beautiful. You feel completely safe. You look around and see all the lush greenery and wildflowers, small animals, and birds which fill the air with their song. There is a smooth breeze and a lovely smell that calms you. You notice something up in the trees and look straight up. In the sky above the trees, you see a spiritual being—it can be anything or anyone. Trust this first image you see. Who or what is it? Take a moment or two to drink in all the details of their high vibration and presence. You feel elevated, and you know this is a meaningful connection happening to you. You ask permission to ask them a question. It can be any question you really need an answer to; or it can be wide open, as in "Please show me what I need to be aware of right now for my greatest good." Take a few minutes to really hear or somehow receive their message. When you feel it is complete, then you can see yourself leaving them a small offering and thanking them for their presence in your life as your spirit guide. Allow yourself to feel any emotions that come, and let them pass through you easily and effortlessly.

You have been visited by three of your spirit guides. You can start to walk back to the path, and then continue forward farther into the forest. Continue walking and feeling how full your heart is with this connection to your guides. You see a gate at the end of the path. You open it and walk through, and you are back in the present moment. Wiggle your fingers and toes, stretch your neck gently, and open your eyes, looking around the room. Come back to the present moment. Take some time to write down what you've just experienced and how you will make sense of the messages you've received.

CHAPTER 11

Angels and Saints

MEDIUMS BELIEVE THAT ANYONE CAN ACCESS any angel or saint, regardless of whether it falls within your religion, or even if you're not religious at all. Although the angels in the examples below may seem aligned with Christian tradition, anyone can access them, and you may recognize their names and energies in multiple faiths. Many angelic presences from Judeo-Christian tradition have equivalents in other traditions, or beings whose functions are similar. For example, in Santeria the Archangel Michael is normally associated with the orisha Ogun. In Buddhism, *devas* have a role similar to angels but are thought to be energies of bodhisattvas or other enlightened ones. Angels and saints—higher beings who can offer guidance—are found across many different cultures throughout history and the world.

It's quite common for mediums to connect to the angelic realm during a reading. Some of us have personal experience or connection to a specific angel, who helps guide the work and clears negative energy or helps the healing process. Usually we call the four Archangels—Michael, Raphael, Gabriel, and Uriel—and many add Metatron to help clear and usher the energy back to source.

Who Are the Archangels?

* Archangel Michael: His color is blue, he carries his sword of light, and he is considered to be a warrior angel, the leader of all the angels and God's armies.

* Archangel Gabriel: His color is white, and he is considered to be the messenger.

* Archangel Raphael: His color is green, and he is considered to be the healer.

* Archangel Uriel: His color is purple, and he is the peacemaker.

* Archangel Metatron: His colors are purple and green, and he is invoked when doing healing work or clearing any negative energies or beliefs.

Throughout history, people have depicted visitations from angels and saints. Some early claims of direct contact were investigated by the church, and the veracity of these experiences were enthusiastically debated among the clergy. Nowadays, we're so much more comfortable believing and experiencing angelic contact for ourselves, without any official stamp of approval. Angelic contact can be very comforting and useful. Many people pray to the Archangels and certain saints for protection, love, lost objects—you name it.

I had a direct experience sighting Archangel Michael once, back in 2007. I was at midnight mass at the Church of Saint Andrew and Saint Paul in downtown Montreal, caroling with a group of friends. It was packed to capacity and there was a very strong, affirming energy that night. I felt very connected to everyone, feeling a oneness that I rarely experienced in the city. At one point, I was singing along and saw an angel appear, standing in the church. He was blond, and he was two stories high. I was awestruck. I kept blinking my eyes over and over again, asking myself, "Is this for real?" And the angel, who I understood to be Archangel Michael, stood there for several minutes before disappearing again. It gives me chills to recall that night. I was already beginning to incorporate Michael into my work, but after that night I'd been visited, and he was now part of my life too.

Flash-forward to 2019. I was in England and found myself in two sacred locations that were associated with Michael, on his ley line. What are ley lines, you ask? This discovery is so fascinating! In 1921, an amateur archaeologist named Alfred Watkins propounded the hypothesis that there are straight lines of energy that link up certain monuments on the planet. There are ley lines associated with certain angels, Mother Mary, and gods like Apollo or Athena, among many others. As Watkins wrote, "Stretching from the southern tip of Ireland, all the way to Israel, there is a straight line that connects seven different landforms that bear the name 'Michael,' or some form of it." These are called "ley lines." The first one I encountered was the Glastonbury Tor, a hill in Somerset known to be sacred due to its association with both Christian and pagan history. The Tor is aligned with the King of the Fairies, Annwn, and is supposedly a gateway into the land of the dead. I knew I wanted to go see the Tor and the Chalice Well at its base, another site said to be full of spiritual power. I'd been wearing a pendant of the Chalice Well symbol for years—a portal to other worlds. I wanted to go see it live; and as I explored Glastonbury and saw the Tor, I felt a strong connection. However, it wasn't until I arrived that I found out it had been built as a tribute to Archangel Michael.

The Tor is the only thing that remains of two churches built for Michael as early as the eleventh and twelfth centuries. However, evidence of Roman pottery and Neolithic tools found during excavations shows it's been in use much longer. The Tor was called The Isle of Avalon, the same as the magical isle in Arthurian legends, and could have been an extension of Glastonbury Abbey, where the labeled coffins of King Arthur and Queen Guinevere were discovered in 1191. You can see why there is so much richness in this monument. Some scholars still question the veracity of this history, but the magic and complexity of this ancient site are palpable to any who visit it.

As I climbed the hill to the Tor that day in 2019, I felt I'd stepped over a force field of some sort. I felt a distinct line or border, and I felt elevated after crossing it. It wasn't until later in my trip that I learned about the ley lines, but I had felt their power while up there. You'll often find monuments and churches built to Saint Michael where there is thought to be evil, because he has the light and power to remove it.

Sightings of angels represent a long tradition of spirit contact. You may have felt an angelic presence around yourself in your life at some moment of vulnerability. If you are open to these presences, they can be life-changing. Just as my own spirit guide shows up in readings and clearings, so too does Archangel Michael. He brings light and cuts away cords and energies of anything negative or evil. In this case, I do summon his help on purpose. Almost everyone I've worked with over the years tells me that when I call him in, they can feel warmth, light, tingling, or the alleviation of symptoms if they have an illness or injury.

Do Our Loved Ones Become Angels?

When our loved ones cross over, do they become angels? The answer is that they can, but it depends on the evolution of their soul. Merely passing through the veil and dying doesn't automatically make someone an angel. In some cases, it might happen if the person's spiritual evolution was at its peak on the Earth, because becoming an angel is the culmination of a long process. People want their loved ones to be ascended angels or celestial intermediaries right away, but it doesn't happen to everyone, nor should it. However, sometimes exceptional people or children—not because they are children, but because of their level of joy and benevolence during their own suffering if they died young—show a very high level of soul evolution. The average person needs to process a life lived with lots of suppressed emotion and sublimated needs, wounds which must be healed in order to ascend. Most of us may come back in other lives to serve before there is an angelic incarnation. However, there are definitely those who do ascend immediately after their life is over. It is also said that animals can do this more quickly than most humans, if they were faithful and in service to their masters—for example, a seeing-eye dog often returns in an angelic form.

CHAPTER 12

Gods and Deities

FOR SOME MEDIUMS, THEIR MAIN GUIDES ARE
gods or deities. These presences can be incredibly demanding
and exhausting, which is why having a god or other deity as a guide is
less common than some of the other spirits mentioned in this book.

I have only had one experience of encountering godly energy. I
was in a vulnerable place and felt that I needed someone to protect
me. I found myself suddenly very attracted to the goddess Kali. She
didn't really appear to me as my guide did, as a strong and distinct
presence, but I was constantly compelled by her image and felt that I
had to learn about her. In this case, I did deliberately invoke her to help
me. I felt that my situation required a very powerful, pure feminine
power to keep the negative energies in my life at bay. I had her *yantra*,
a mystical diagram celebrated in Tantric tradition, on my door, and I
prayed to her. In return, her energy helped me stay strong and change
my life, moving out of a bad apartment in a high-crime area and taking the steps necessary to improve my situation. After that, I felt no
need to keep calling on her, so her presence fell away gently from my
life. Guides, angels, and deities do come in and out temporarily when
we need them. I prayed to Kali for about three years, and only to her.

If you are also compelled by a deity or god and want to work with those energies, I would only suggest that you treat the practice like a long-term committed relationship and less like a Tinder date. Get to know your guide's energy over time: it really won't work otherwise.

Encounter with the Goddess

Kaya was on vacation with her friend in California and saw a poster advertising a goddess ritual on the beach that night. Kaya was always a bit of a skeptic when it came to spiritual groups and gatherings, but her friend was so enthusiastic about trying it that she said yes. On her way to the beach, she noticed the people participating in the ritual starting to congregate around a lit fire pit. Many of the people were wearing loose clothing, almost robes or flowing dresses, and some had flowers in their hair. She thought it was pretty cheesy at first glance. A woman in a white flowing tunic finally stepped forward and introduced herself as the guide for that evening. Everyone clapped and seemed to know her.

Kaya only found out later that this was a special date for the group, and the invocation of the goddess was sacred to their practice. As the ritual began, they were all guided to stretch and sway a bit, and dance if they desired to dance. The guide led them into breathwork and then instructed them to begin moving around the fire as she chanted mantras and drummed. Kaya felt super-awkward at first; but as the breath and movement kicked in, and the atmosphere of the fire pit and drums pulsed through her, it started to feel very good—freeing, even. After a while, as the group continued to move and chant, the guide asked everyone to find a spot and sit around the fire. She told them to close their eyes, and she began the incantation to the goddess.

All at once, Kaya felt the most beautiful, pure love envelop her. It was as if she was being hugged by the most nurturing mother imaginable. She opened her eyes slightly to gaze at the fire and felt a presence growing stronger. Kaya felt her logical side dimly in the background, wanting to dismiss this all as a fantasy, but she couldn't deny the soothing energy that had shifted her whole body into calmness.

After the ritual ended, Kaya made sure to speak to the guide and ask her more about what had happened. The guide explained that the group had been calling upon the energy of the Divine Feminine, and told Kaya more about how to access this power on her own. Once Kaya knew that the energy of the goddess was real and knew that she could call on it again, she began a relationship with it as a spirit guide that became very comforting and beautiful.

Calling on the Divine Feminine

One way to connect to the Divine Feminine energy yourself is to nurture yourself. Nurturing is a deeper word than self-care, which is such a trendy term these days. Self-care might be a bath with essential oils and Epsom salts and then nice, calming music before bed—which is pleasant, but it doesn't fully address the deep emotional care and presence represented in the Divine Feminine, or Divine Mother. Self-care is sometimes spoken of as a set of tasks, instead of a practice of forgiving, loving behavior toward ourselves. Nurturing is ultra-tender and fully connected emotionally. If you need a bit of help to get into that vibration, you can try the exercise below.

Connecting to the Divine Feminine

Find your favorite blanket—you know, the warmest, softest one you have, the one that makes you feel like curling up and napping in it. Then take a moment to choose a fragrance that makes you feel very safe and comforted. You might like lavender oil, or you could make an aromatic drink like a cup of hot cocoa, or apple cider with cinnamon. Dim the lights or turn them off and then light a candle in the room you will rest in for this exercise. Make sure there will be no interruptions or annoyances. You might want to turn off your phone or your Wi-Fi.

Lie down in a comfortable position under your blanket and with a pillow or even a teddy bear if you wish, and get into a cozy position. We're creating a womb-like environment for you to let go and feel completely safe and cared for. When you're ready, start breathing a bit more slowly. See if you can feel the subtlety of your breath on your upper lip, or the hot and cold of the in-breath and the out-breath.

Next, I want you to visualize yourself as being inside a beautiful protective sphere of light. Nothing can penetrate this sphere unless you give it permission. See it around you everywhere and notice how big it is, what color it is, and so forth. Imagine that this sphere is an energetic womb where you are utterly safe. You can say that to yourself a few times: "I am safe," "I am protected," "I am loved."

Now imagine the most nurturing presence you can conjure. For some, this might be your own mom, and for others it might be someone else you see as a perfect mother. This is your Divine Mother in some form. Imagine that she is coming to you and hears everything that you need right now. She is gently caressing your head and hair. She puts her hand on your chest and asks you, "What do you need, my dear?" Visualize her giving this to you. Be totally open to your intuition, the symbols and colors you see, your emotions, your worthiness to receive all that you need. In your mind or out loud, say, "I surrender to the Divine and receive all my blessings and guidance with gratitude."

Take a few moments to thank this Divine Feminine presence in your life, knowing you can call on her always. You might want to stay under your blanket and nap, sip some water, or do some gentle stretches. Stay in this energy or mode and move slowly. Don't rush back into your day or tasks. Be calm, slow, and receptive to how you now perceive yourself and your environment when feeling loved and safe.

CHAPTER 13

Child Spirits

SOMETIMES OUR GUIDES ARE CHILDREN—PAST, present, and future. They may be children from a time before you were born, or children who have departed within your lifetime. Sometimes we are even visited by the soul of a future child on the way.

While I haven't had my own children to verify this, a friend of mine, who is a very strong and accurate medium, had an interesting experience with the energy of a future child. This friend, who already had two sons, felt her pregnancy in advance, well before it happened. In fact, we both felt the vibration of pregnancy a year before she conceived. We also both felt that a boy was coming. Her experience was so fascinating to me. Before she officially became pregnant, she started to see the soul of a little boy floating around her. After her pregnancy was confirmed, this spirit was still there. After another two or three months passed, she suddenly saw another soul floating around her, another boy. The two spirits stayed there for a few weeks, and then she felt one of them choose to become her son—the other disappeared. She believed that the soul of the spirit who had chosen her became her son around four or five months into her pregnancy.

Sometimes the child spirit you encounter will become your own child, but other times it is a child guide that comes through to you. There are all kinds of child guides. If a child spirit guide is around you, it can mean a few things. It may be that what your own soul needs right now is the guidance of a young, joyful, curious, or innocent spirit to help you restore your own inner joy and wonder. At other times, you might encounter your own inner child. In that case, you might see a younger version of yourself around you at an age you need to revisit in order to heal or resolve something. Let's take a closer look.

Child Guides

If your spirit guide is a child, there is a special kind of relationship and way to speak with this guide. They will speak to you through your own inner-child wisdom and help you heal. This isn't the old, sage vibe we encounter when spirit guides appear in books or movies; this is more of a wise-yet-curious spirit. A child spirit is full of knowledge, but is still hungry to learn and excited about the world. This might happen like this:

You are on your usual route to work one day, and in a flash you see an image of a kid outside your passenger window on a bicycle. You keep driving but are a bit distracted by this vision and keep checking to see if it is still there. Sure enough, every time you look out the passenger window, you see this image of a child about nine years old riding a bike and enjoying it. You're suddenly very curious as to why this kid is there, and you look at your usual boring route in a whole new way. As you pass the old donut shop you used to go to that is now a car dealership, you feel nostalgia for that time and remember how you felt life was easier then. You glance outside again, and the kid is stopping the bike right at the donut shop driveway. You're not normally like this, but you are now curious enough to double back around the block and stop at the old shop and park the car. You see the kid smiling and sitting on his bike right next to the door, and you get the feeling you're supposed to go inside. You're not so sure about this, but you go in anyway and suddenly recognize someone you haven't seen in ages working at the counter. It's a happy recognition, and you both smile and start talking. When you glance toward where you saw the child, you see they are also smiling. A reunion has happened. It was innocent, but it was profound as well.

Don't be surprised if this kind of guide shows you your childhood memories as messages. They may lead you to places or even music or toys you used to love, or speak to you symbolically. This kind of message will be soft and simple like a child, but will really hit home on an emotional level. Make no mistake—the wisdom a child spirit imparts will have just as much impact as any other kind of spirit guide. Maybe more!

Souls of Future Children

Many women feel a presence of their future child long before they get pregnant. I've encountered friends, clients, and fellow mediums who have told me that they dreamed of a baby or small child in their mind's eye before conceiving. Some could describe the kind of personality the child would have, and in many cases found that this premonition became reality. It's an interesting lesson about how the soul works, because if a child's spirit comes to a mother before conception, then hovers around her before entering her body fully during the pregnancy at around four or five months—which is pretty accurate from the accounts I've heard—it tells us that this soul can also move on to new parents if the pregnancy doesn't come to fruition, which is a great comfort to many I've met who've lost children to miscarriages.

If you are pregnant or trying to conceive, you can trust that the soul of the child meant for you is around, and you can start to communicate with it. You can do this by doing a mental scan to see if you see anything floating around you like my friend did. Sometimes you'll be able to feel there is someone there, a feeling that you're not alone. If that happens, you can ask this presence, "Are you my child?" You can get an intuitive answer, even if you have to ask a few times.

If you have a child who is nonverbal or very introverted, you can also use these techniques to communicate on another level with them. When using this technique, it's important that you learn to drop into your heart, not your head. Place your hand on your heart if you need to and start to breathe and feel from there. See the cord or the light that connects you to your child and vice versa. If you see it clearly, then strengthen that bond by adding more light to it, more colors, making it a bit larger. You can mentally send your child anything you have in your heart and speak to them through your heart energy as opposed to your spoken words. Children and animals function this way. We have to reach them through a heart-to-heart connection.

If you're not able to see a light or cord of attachment between your child and yourself, then you can build one. Be gentle when you do this. Slowly see a beautiful warm light coming from your heart and slowly see it reaching theirs. Be patient with this; but when that cord is there and flowing, you will both feel a bond and stronger connection than ever. This works with anyone who is difficult or impossible to speak to, so it certainly works with our fur babies too.

CHAPTER 14

Pet Spirits

MANY OF US KNOW THAT OUR PETS CAN SEE AND sense spirits. Your cat keeps staring at a blank wall, or your dog barks and gets excited every time he is in a certain corner of a room. Animals aren't disconnected from their intuition and can have a full sensory experience of the world around them. They can see spirits, sense entities and bad energy, feel how we hurt even when we don't say it, and reflect those emotions back to us, for those able to receive that energy. In this way, animals can function as spirit guides while they're living in this world.

My cat Gen showed me all these capacities and more. She would meow at a wall in my apartment all the time. There was absolutely nothing there. Other times, she would be tracking something flying around, so I'd look to see if there was a bug in the house—of course, there was nothing there. Her head would do sudden ninety-degree turns, zipping back and forth faster than anything can fly. It was then that I realized she was seeing energy or spirits.

At one point there were nine cats living at the pagan shop where I worked, so you can imagine how many of them were guides. One cat in particular, Gulliver, sat up on his hind legs and winked at me the day

I applied for the job. He became my best bud while I worked there. He would walk across the table and lie down on the tarot cards at the end of a reading when a customer's time was up—he was like an orange tabby clock. He comforted people, and he indicated who he liked and didn't. There were always one or two of the cats who slept in the readers' corner all day, helping us out. Tequila, who was named because he was a kitten found in a tequila box and taken into the store by the owner, would come upstairs before my workshops and walk clockwise around the circle of chairs I had set up, essentially performing a space-clearing ritual before my psychic development class.

Pets can also give us messages telling us that our departed loved ones are around us. Your cat may suddenly want to go to sleep on your grandma's favorite blanket all the time, or even remove a photo from out of a book on your shelf. Don't laugh—my cat Willow has managed to pull documents out of a tightly packed bookshelf to show me. Your dog might bark and turn in circles beside your grandpa's favorite tree in the yard. We have to home in on these behaviors and ask ourselves if we also sense a presence at that moment. Our pets are spiritual guides if we open up to them, and can help us on our healing journey.

When we lose a pet, it's always devastating for us. Most of us dream of our lost pets at some point, and these dreams can be opportunities for their spirits to let us know they are okay. Outside of dreams, their energies may also linger after their passing, and we may feel them in the room with us, on the bed, meowing or barking in a hallway or a garage. Pet spirits can give us messages just as human spirits do. Maybe their toy appears out of nowhere one day, sitting in the middle of the kitchen floor, or you're meeting someone new and your pet appears in your mind with a behavior that lets you know whether they like this person or not.

When our pets, living or departed, communicate these energies, are you listening? Have you felt your dog or cat sense a spiritual presence? Pay attention. They can help keep our relationships and homes flowing with the right energy.

Pets as Living Spirit Guides or Familiars

A little orange tabby cat was roaming around a house that was for sale when Selina saw him. She was there to stage the house, and one of the contractors working on it came and asked, "Hey, do you want a cat?" She said, "No, thanks." She felt she had enough responsibilities in her life as it was. The cat kept meowing and roaming around all day, regardless of their trying to remove him. When Selina got in her car at the end of the day, she turned and saw that this little orange cat was on the car seat. It seemed almost impossible, since the window was barely open and it didn't seem like there would have been enough space for him to shimmy through—but somehow he had. She found this such a miracle that she decided to adopt him and called him Jesus.

This cat now roams the building she lives in and visits those who need him. He stands up on his hind legs, and with both front paws together he makes a motion almost as if he is praying. He has done this in very meaningful moments, such as the day Selina's friend came over in tears after a breakup. At the very moment Selina's friend looked at her and said, "I don't know if I'll ever love again," there was Jesus beside her, praying, then rubbing against her. She always felt that this was a sign not to give up hope on love.

After I moved into my office, which is a small flat in a residential area, I was visited one day by a fluffy black cat. He announced himself with a loud meow and walked up the stairs to my studio. He let me hold him and hug him right away, and I was in love but also wondered if he had an owner. After I asked around in the area, I found out that the cat, named Scarlet, was the neighborhood's cat, at least according to the man who technically owns him. Scarlet visits those who need him. He came to me all summer that year. He also spent a lot of time climbing in the window of another neighbor who was having lots of back pain, who told me that the cat's presence brought him a lot of comfort, both emotional and physical.

One day I had a client come in. She was a fascinating person full of stories and spunk. She had courageously broken the rules in life in ways that helped others and had a very full life. Now in her seventies, she had an inoperable tumor in one eye. She and I had just begun our session when Scarlet announced himself at the landing. I asked my client if she was okay with Scarlet coming in, and she said she loved cats. He walked straight over to the table, jumped up, and head-butted her eye—the one with the tumor. This all happened within two minutes of his arrival. We were both amazed. Cats are messengers and healers if we are open to them—and this woman was very touched by his gesture. He knew exactly where her pain was. She felt he was saying that she was very loved, even as she felt vulnerable due to her physical ailment. They cuddled for the rest of the reading.

Pet Visitations

....

Many people feel their pets have come to them after they passed. My client Susan once told me she felt her dog on her bed every night for months after he departed, and she did not feel his presence in a purely energetic way—the bed had actually seemed to sink down in the place where he had formerly slept. Another friend, Karen, told me that her cat used to appear to her as a vision when something was important. One time, her cat appeared like an apparition at the top of a staircase, so she took it as a sign to be careful on the stairs; and sure enough, she later found that one of the steps was loose and could have caused her to trip and fall. Stories like this abound: so, for me, pet visitations are completely common and real.

CHAPTER 15

Animal Totems

B ELIEF IN ANIMAL TOTEMS HAS ITS ROOTS IN
indigenous practice and can be enormously powerful. Animals
can be spirit guides. They can be living animals you encounter, or
they can come to you in dreams. Some animals have come into your
life since birth and are always walking with you as your main guide.
Others will show up as temporary helpers and messengers. Sometimes
your guide will be your former pet, but any animal can be a totem. I
have never encountered a gorilla except at a zoo and hadn't seen one
live until the age four or five; yet my relationship to them in dreams
is strong, and I dream about them often.

Based on the nature of the animal that appears to you, whether you
see it alive in nature, in a significant dream, or popping up synchro-
nistically in books, movies, or other representations such as art or
toys—the animal that is showing itself to you can be a great source of
wisdom. Let's say, for example, that you dream of a buffalo. Buffalos are
known for their strength and size, and for their commitment to their
herd. Groups of enormous buffalo traveling together are incredible
in their capacity to withstand attacks from predators. But to discern
the message that this animal may be showing you, it's important to

determine what it was doing when you saw it. Was the buffalo angry, defending itself, eating, breeding, at peace, or in pain? It all means something. Look at the nature of a buffalo and think about how you can apply the central features of its nature to yourself: recognize that you may have these qualities or should develop them, for example. Say you dreamed of a buffalo standing still as a rainstorm began, holding its ground as all the other animals ran for cover. This is a hugely symbolic insight! This could be a message for you to channel the strength of the buffalo: to not hide, but face whatever storm that dream is showing you.

I have had a few encounters with a crow spirit, and so have many of my clients. A friend of mine makes smudging wands from feathers she finds and adds beautiful gemstones. She agreed to lead me to a place where she used to find crow feathers because I'd been encountering them more and wanted to work more with their medicine. She led me to a park area near some train tracks that weren't in use anymore. What we found that day was a graveyard of crows. It was shocking, but it confirmed what I already knew about crows bringing about transformation.

Crows show up when your life is going through a cycle of death and rebirth. They are clever, aware, and connected to the mysteries of life and death. When I encountered the graveyard of crows with my friend, I already had daily contact with these animals. Crows flew around my apartment building all the time, plus I lived near a cemetery where they also liked to congregate. On a day soon after our discovery, I was walking and thinking about the possibility of moving out of the city and toward the waterfront when two huge crows circled me, their feathers practically brushing my body. I was hit with a wave of certainty that I would have to move, for my own well-being. Moving was a huge decision for me, particularly because it meant recognizing that the many hopes and dreams I'd had for my life in Montreal just hadn't happened, so to let go somehow felt like I'd failed. Although I felt so certain after my encounter with the circling crows, it still took about a year to make peace with the fact that I needed to live near water and in a smaller village for my soul to be happy. But in the end, it was the best decision I'd made in years, even though it took a lot of deliberating—and during that time period, crows continued showing up in odd and serendipitous ways. Crows both living and deceased can affirm the end of a chapter in your life.

Another client of mine had a similar experience. She was about to end a long-term marriage and the way of life that had accompanied it, but didn't know it at first. She just kept seeing crows on her property. Crows even laid eggs in nests on her lawn, and baby crows were born there. Within a year, she was divorced and moved out to a new home. I've heard many stories like this. No matter what animal shows up, pay close attention to its character traits, mating habits, the food it likes, cycles of time that apply to it—all of it has meaning. And if you want to read more, the best book for reference and study is *Animal Speak* by Ted Andrews.

Chris and the Owl

A friend of mine named Chris once came face to face with an owl—very rare in our city. He knew about totems, so the encounter was very meaningful to him. After that first meeting, he began to come across owls multiple times in a short period of time—not only the live encounter, but images of owls also began showing up in other significant moments. He felt like he was consistently seeing owls on TV, in books, on fabrics, and so on as if they were trying to communicate with him. He knew at that point that he had to honor the observations, and chose to see it as an affirmation of the wise and spiritual side of himself, and an encouragement to develop this part of his personality.

Louise and the Bat

Louise returned to her office after not being there for a week or so. It was time to tidy it up. She was sitting on her couch when a framed piece of art on the wall behind it suddenly fell. When she got up to put it back in position, she found a dead bat behind it! Obviously startled, she looked up bat symbolism right away after removing the body of the animal safely from the space. As she learned, the bat is a totem representing major changes ahead, and is also an encouragement to trust your intuition. It can also mean that it is time to have the courage to face the darkness. Because the bat was dead, Louise knew its presence was a further message of a death and rebirth to come in her life. In the few weeks that followed, her insight was proved to be correct: her relationship with her mother changed drastically, and she also weathered a major health issue. All was good in the end, but it was a wake-up call for her! The bat heralded a new awareness that life can change at any moment, which requires bravery and trust in your own mind.

Butterflies

....

Butterflies are a classic and beautiful totem for transformation. People often report seeing butterflies when the spirits of departed loved ones are present, and butterflies frequently serve as messages from spirit guides. The butterfly as totem can carry a message from your loved one or guide, or it may *be* the guide itself. Butterfly symbolism is fairly obvious, but still so powerful: it's all about figuring out what stage you are in your transformation. Are you needing to cocoon before you spread your wings? Or is it time to come out and fly?

CHAPTER 16

Interdimensional Beings

WHEN I SAY, "INTERDIMENSIONAL BEINGS," I'm using a broad umbrella term for a group of entities that can include fairies, elves, gnomes, Pleiadeans, Arcturians, aliens of all kinds, mothmen, poltergeists, reptilians, time travelers, ascended masters, and more. Mediums like Esther Hicks and Jane Roberts channel interdimensional beings with wisdom to impart. I had an apartment that had a portal in the closet (see page 123). The being that came through there as a brief guide for me was also an interdimensional being, not of Earth.

It is more common now to hear people say they too feel they are from another dimension, and this is their first incarnation on Earth. Many who call themselves Starseeds say they came from the Pleiades, for example. They long for a home that doesn't exist here on this planet, and they have very high sensitivity. So many people have also had alien encounters or even a sense of being abducted or experimented on as they sleep. Others when they connect to their spirit guides discover they are from another dimension as well.

What Are Interdimensional Beings?

....

These are beings who dwell in a different or parallel dimension to ours. Some are time travelers; some are fairies, elves, or gnomes. Some interdimensional beings are aliens, or from different star systems. Many people currently identify as Starseeds—beings who originated from either the Pleiades, Arcturus, or Orion. Some are called Indigo Children or Crystal Children. These are thought to have had their previous lives in other dimensions and are now reincarnating here on Earth for the first time. Some spirits such as my guide can be said to be interdimensional as well, since they are time travelers. Any of these beings can come through to you in your life as a guide or messenger once, or some might be your constant spirit guide.

The wide range of interdimensional beings can be a bit overwhelming to us at first. Everyone has their niche in terms of which beings and worlds they feel connected to. And some skeptics may be sensitive to those who say they've encountered a fairy or saw a mothman—it's definitely a gray area in which some people will question your experiences. However, remember that these beings and the lore surrounding them have been around for centuries. While working at the pagan shop, I heard these sorts of stories all the time. And when I went to the United Kingdom, I heard stories about what I am calling interdimensional beings *everywhere*—the respect for the fairies over there is real.

Some of these entities can be quite terrifying to see, and others may make you question if you've been watching too many *Star Trek* or Disney movies; but if you have a meaningful dream, vision, or pattern of encounters with an interdimensional being, don't write them off immediately. Learn the lore behind the creatures you have seen, just as you would an animal totem, and try to see what it is trying to teach you. Some of these beings will feel like wise sages and others can be tricksters or downright scary—such as the reptilians, which are rumored to shapeshift and have been associated with all manner of conflict. Just as in science fiction like *Star Trek,* some alien races are benevolent; others, not so much.

My Closet Portal

I once lived in an apartment with an incredible amount of spirit activity. It was a two-bedroom apartment, but it felt like a five-bedroom. It's a bit hard to describe, but there were so many ways this space was divided—energetically, not by walls—that it felt ten times bigger than it was. I even hosted parties in there, and I never do that anywhere else.

I found that there was at least one distinct spirit presence in the space. A priest walked around one half of the apartment, just keeping an eye on things. He was harmless, but he was there on some sort of mission. I have no idea how long he'd been there or who might have sent him; and I didn't ask him about it or try to remove him, because I felt he was protecting the apartment somehow. He only walked through one room and the hallway.

Then there was a closet portal in the bedroom. No matter what I did to arrange it, close it, open it up wide, use herbs, you name it—this closet felt like a freight train that never stopped. One night, I saw something come out of the closet and sit by my left foot in the bed.

He was about four feet tall and stocky; he moved in an awkward way; and when he spoke, it was hard to understand what he was saying. All I ever got from him what that he was from another dimension, a Starseed, but I wasn't able to truly identify which one. Both of these spirits stayed in that apartment after I left.

Encountering Darker Forces

No one really wants to see the darker forces at work, but the Universe is made up of both dark and light. If you think you may be encountering more malevolent energies, there are a few distinguishing features that can help you confirm what you're dealing with. The first is that the person or the vibe of a place will give you a cold chill throughout your body. If there is something negative in the home where an entity might be dwelling, or in the person who might be carrying its energy, the coldness can be palpable—some even say it's like an icy breeze with no discernible source.

The second thing to look out for is a pervasive feeling of discomfort, anything from some generalized anxiety around a place to actual physical pain. This could manifest in chest pressure, difficulty breathing, or feeling a bit weak or nauseated. If your primary vibe of a place or person gives you these strong sensations, all I can tell you is to avoid them and get out! It's the old airplane adage—put on your own oxygen mask or life jacket before saving others. In this case, we need to remove ourselves from the scene or person and *then* use our light and cleansing techniques to address the problem. I realize that my admonition to run as soon as you can probably sounds scary or alarmist, but I've seen far too many people adversely affected by negative energy or malevolent entities. Trust those sensations and protect your energy.

Encounters with Fairies

According to *The Irish Times*, "... the fairies of Ireland are not the magical or elaborate fairies that we know from stories such as Cinderella or Peter Pan or the paintings created by Victorian and Edwardian artists such as Richard Dadd and Edward Robert Hughes or the photographs of the Cottingley Fairies taken by Elsie Wright and Frances Griffiths during the reign of King George V, nor are they the delicate sweet fairies we see in a Disney film." No, these fairies are more akin to the creatures in an Edgar Allan Poe story! Real fairies are known to do real damage—they can be very mischievous or full of tricks, but also can be angered and become vengeful if not treated with care. Some believe that fairies caused the Great Potato Famine in Ireland, after all. These creatures are both revered and feared in the United Kingdom. So, how do you keep them from doing evil? They usually want offerings, perhaps bread or other food. In exchange, they can assist your luck and will be less likely to play tricks on you. Treat them respectfully, and their presence can invite good fortune—get on their bad side, and they'll make your life very difficult.

Ascended Masters

You will see many mediums who channel the ascended masters. These might be Buddha, Quan Yin, Jesus, Mother Mary, Sanat Kumara, Maitreya, Confucius, or Saint Germain, to name a few. These are people who had a simple life or incarnation here on Earth but went through significant spiritual tests and transformations before ascending; therefore, they can be called on to guide us in their wisdom now. Their energy is so vast that they can be present to many all at once. Unlike an ancestor guide, the connection you'll have with them is less of a personal relationship. Anyone can call upon them at any time.

If you have an experience of an ascended master on your spiritual journey, it will be memorable. You will suddenly have access to high levels of wisdom. An ascended master will assist you more in terms of helping the evolution of yourself and your family line and karma in this life, and the healing of humanity at large. It's a big picture that they impart to us.

They also will grant you awareness and access to spiritual truths of the cosmos. You may encounter their presence and be so filled with love or joy in a way you've never felt, because the Universe is love. You might be meditating when you see a master show you a diagram or visual of something about space, or a global chart of something. It's always very individual what information you are shown, but the context with an ascended master is the broad view of humanity, not the mundane questions of life. It's very special.

CHAPTER 17

Entities

WE TOUCHED UPON THIS BRIEFLY IN THE LAST section; but as we reach into the spirit realm, it's possible that we may encounter darker forces, interdimensional or not. Sometimes we have to speak of the nastier things in life in order to understand and protect ourselves from them. Entities are real, and evil is real. It doesn't mean we have to succumb to it and that we are powerless against it—but we do need to be able to spot evil when it enters our life. There are certain patterns I have seen that let me know there is an entity present in a place, around a person, or attached to an object. Possession is also real, although less common. My goal in writing this part of the book is to help you identify signs of this kind of energy so you can cleanse and clear it to protect yourself. This information is not meant to scare you, although I realize it might. As an analogy, imagine going through life without telling your kids that they can't trust just anyone. It's not a pleasant reality for them to enter—to know that not everyone is safe—but they have to know it in order to prevent bad things from happening. It's the same thing spiritually.

Have you ever felt a cold chill pass through you when you met someone, or a experienced a feeling of dread as you walked across a room? Have you ever lived somewhere and found that there were areas of the house you never wanted to enter? Are there places in your current home that are constantly cluttered or seem to have a feeling of being unresolved? And on top of that, does the temperature drop when you're in that area? These are all signs of a presence. It doesn't mean it's evil, so don't be scared right away; but it does mean that something is stuck there and needs clearing. I have been brought into all kinds of homes and businesses to clear spiritual energies and have seen all kinds of things. These presences can represent something deeply entrenched that needs a lot of work, and other times it can be released quickly. Sometimes the energy that is trapped is a ghost, a lost soul, or an imprint of events that happened in a place.

An entity might present as an angry, anxious energy. Its presence can sometimes feel like something is near you—particularly behind you or on the left-hand side of your body. It might feel like a presence trying to sit on your bed at night, touch you without asking, or press wordlessly on your chest. These are signs of a dark entity around you; and if you experience them, they must be addressed.

Remember the trip to Sedona I mentioned, where a medium saw something attached to my back? And then the Reiki master saw it too? At the time, that medium mentioned all this to me while standing in the lunch line at the Grand Canyon, and I had a sudden flashback to the moment the entity entered me. I remember how odd it felt. It was sort of like when you swallow a mouthful of food that you know you won't digest well. At the time, it was the middle of my day, and I was with clients, so I had no time to stop and check in with myself and process what had happened. I also hadn't had any previous experience with this, and so I wasn't equipped to know if this presence was still inside me, or what to do. What I can tell you in hindsight, though, is that I had had back pain in that area for years, and I had a struggle with darker thoughts during those years too. Everything was removed while I was in Sedona, and by the end of the trip I looked like a new person. Entities are real; and sudden changes in behavior, unexpected "bad luck," pockets of cold, and clutter or negative vibes in your home can all be signs.

When you speak to any spirit, it should always keep a respectful space from you just as people would here in life. When anything comes at you from behind or on your left side, be careful. When you are touched with the spirit asking or it feels invasive, clear this energy. If anything speaks quickly, angrily, or tells you what to do—do not listen. These are classic signs of lower energies. When a spirit is in the light— be it an ancestor or angel, animal totem, pet spirit, or otherwise—it will approach you gently, keep its distance, ask permission to make contact, speak with minimal words or gestures, and mainly—it will *feel good*. Any messages that provoke fear or doubt, or confuse you and prompt you to overanalyze—do not listen. The light never speaks to us that way. Beings in the light speak in ways that give us peace, clarity, and reassurance. They leave us feeling stronger.

Encountering a Succubus or Incubus

This is a really tricky form of entity because it comes to you in a sensual or sexual way, thus it is harder to spot or resist. A succubus is a female demonic entity that has sex with men during their sleep. They are said to prey on emotionally weak men and steal their souls. An incubus is the male version. These stories are also pretty common, although I would flag them and wonder if the person is truly encountering such a spirit, or if they are experiencing or reliving trauma from a violation of some kind. Still, these seductive or soul-stealing stories are as old as time.

Encountering an Arcturian

On one of my trips to Sedona, my friend Jeff was meditating near the airport. It was commonly understood among mediums that this area contains a vortex where Jeff felt like he would be able to receive some of the more intense masculine energy it has. Sedona is full of vortices of swirling energy, which is why many people flock to it for their spiritual development. I felt it firsthand too. Jeff wanted to attain a higher level in his meditation practice and would sit on the hillside daily, doing his breathing techniques and allowing himself to receive whatever visions or insights came.

One time, in a particularly deep state, Jeff looked off in the distance and saw a humanoid being, which he understood to be an Arcturian. Arcturians are said to be the predecessors of humans and are here to help the Earth heal—they have human-like forms, pale skin, and dark eyes and hair. Jeff saw this being calmly standing before him for several minutes and felt he was receiving downloads of insights about his role on the Earth, as well as theirs. He was told that Arcturus is the midway station for the soul's progression of intelligent beings on Earth, and they use a light craft called a Merkabah—a star tetrahedron, or multipointed star shape (you'll often see crystals in this shape). The Arcturians wanted him to know that we all must realize that the planet is a living being and needs healing. He came away from his meditation that day elated and energized with a sense of purpose. Encounters with interdimensional beings, when they happen, can be deeply moving—not everything we'd call an "entity" is dark or malevolent. In Jeff's case, he was able to connect with an intelligent being and came away with a new understanding of his place in the world.

Part 4

Spiritual Protection

B EFORE COVERING THE MANY WAYS we can protect ourselves spiritually with light, altars, gems, essential oils, and meditation techniques, I would like to say that the strongest and most basic form of spiritual protection we have is our own self-respect and integrity. If you have your sense of self intact and will stand up for yourself, love yourself, and ask for loving ethical treatment in return, this high energy will protect you from many things. A strong sense of self isn't esoteric. It allows you the strength and confidence to delve into the spiritual, the shadow work, the other paradigms of exploration to enrich your life. The suggestions I make here are to help create and strengthen this with a practice or ritual that helps reinforce the self.

CHAPTER 18

Spiritual-Protection Exercise

B EFORE WE GO INTO THE PARTICULARS OF SPIRI-
tual protection, try this simple exercise. This will help you fully
visualize yourself surrounded in clean white light.

First, sit or lie down and get comfortable, breathing deeply.

Visualize a halo or a crown of light around your head.

Scan this crown or halo and see if it is all clean and clear—make
sure it has no spots or missing pieces.

Mentally visualize that it is all clean and whole. Notice any shifts
in your sensation once the halo is fully there.

Bring down a column of light from the Heavens or Source, or just
envision bright sunshine.

See this column of light surround you from head to toe, front and
back, from the top of your head all the way down to your feet.

See the column of light extend downward into the Earth's core.

Say aloud, or think to yourself:

As above, so below.

Let this column of light protect me and cleanse me of all that is not for my highest good.

Anything or anyone, seen or unseen, please be removed from me and go to the light.

Notice how you feel emotionally and physically when you are able to visualize this completely. Most people will feel lighter, aches and pains can disappear, and sudden flashes of insight can come.

This skill is truly all you need.

CHAPTER 19

Altars and Sacred Spaces

A**N ALTAR CAN BE VERY FORMAL, INCLUDING** representations of all elements of the earth; special silk cloths; amulets or statuary of deities, angels, or saints; or more; with everything placed precisely in particular areas. For some, this level of structure and study helps strengthen their practice. For others, their altar might be more casual and intimate: an unplanned collection of objects with personal significance sitting under a favorite tree, a small collection of crystals set out on a nightstand, or a few carefully chosen magical tools sitting on a chair facing an ocean view. Sacred spaces are very important for our healing work. How many of us did not have a sacred space, somewhere that was just ours, untouched by anyone but us, growing up? How many don't have the luxury of space in order to do this now? We may share a sacred space, perhaps in a building like a church or temple, a yoga studio, or a beautiful garden in the city. Even if your space is used by many others in a community, having a sense that it is personal and sacred helps us to reclaim and maintain our uniqueness, our identity. You can create these areas almost anywhere if you get creative.

Growing up, I always longed to escape and have my own sanctuary. The first one I had was a tree swing my dad hung for me in the field behind our house. He cut out all the tall grasses and weeds in the area, and suspended the tire swing from a huge branch. I basically had a treed enclosure to swing in, and I would go out there and sing at the top of my lungs where no one could hear me. It was perfect for a ten-year-old.

As I got older, it wasn't quite enough. I wanted even more privacy because my family could still see the swing from the house. I went down the gravel road, down the hill, and into a ravine to build a treehouse. I could still hear my mom calling through the woods when it was time for dinner, but I had my privacy there. It was great. Similarly, your apartment can be your sacred space if you live alone, and you can design it to reflect your personality. If you personalize your home and make it feel special, then when you enter you will remember who you are. If you don't live alone, you can make your bedroom your sacred space. It may have certain things on the walls that you like, for example, and can make you feel grounded, inspired, and protected. You may consider instituting certain codes of conduct for your space, so that no one may enter it without showing it respect—perhaps the rule is that you can't raise your voice in this space, or that you will greet it as you step across the threshold. You will know instantly who *sees* you and accepts you by their interaction with your space if you invite them into it. Do they follow the rules you've set down? Do they treat it with respect, or do they disregard its importance?

Another way to look at sacred space starts with your own body. You don't always need a physical space, a closet or room—you just need a sense that your body is your temple and a desire to treat it as such. We all have boundaries in terms of what makes us feel comfortable, and we have to respect them and ask others to respect them. It is exactly the same with spirits. Something may come knocking on your door, but you don't have to answer. A spirit may present itself; but if it doesn't show itself to be positive, healthy, or in the light, you don't have to listen or allow it into your sacred space. In this case, the sacred space or altar may even be your own mind, or your aura of awareness, since a spirit usually arrives as an energy, a thought, a perception.

How do we make our own mind a sacred space? One of the best ways to create a sacred space in your own mind is through meditation. Having a practice can keep your mind calm—and it doesn't have to be sitting meditation. If going for a good run keeps your head clear, that's perfect. If singing loudly in your car clears your head, great. It just takes a practice to keep your mind calm and maintain enough detachment so you can perceive when something is in alignment with your energy—or not. When you maintain that kind of detachment, you can make informed choices about whether or not to interact with the energies that you encounter in life, whether they are humans or spirit guides. We need this gentle space in between our own energies and others' to discern what we should allow into our lives. Don't allow just anything or anyone to stay rent-free in your head and make a mess of your psyche and your emotions. The more you have a routine, ritual, sacred practice, or special place to visit and ground yourself, the easier it becomes to remember: *this is me, and this is not me—I can choose what I speak to and allow into my sacred space.*

CHAPTER 20

Herbs and Oils

ACROSS THE WORLD AND EVERY CULTURE, THERE
is some tradition of using certain oils and herbs as medicines
to heal ailments, grant visions, banish evil, invite prosperity, or for
another sacred purpose. When you begin to research these practices,
their permutations can seem endless. Using herbs and oils for protection can be immensely useful, and I'd encourage you to look into
the full spectrum of how they have benefited humans across time and
around the globe. However, you may find it most useful to connect to the
practice that aligns with your ancestors, or the traditions of the land on
which you live now. You may be familiar with Indigenous, Buddhist, or
Hindu traditions of burning herbs like sage for sacred smoke, consuming
Ayurvedic healing elixirs made from oils or plants, or meditating while
burning incense. However, there are many less-known Celtic or Nordic
traditions of burning and using herbs too, as well as practices that date
back to ancient Greece, Italy, South America . . . everywhere, really!

Just as with everything, plants are individual energies and have
properties that are unique, and thus you can develop a relationship to
that plant energy. Over time, there will be certain herbs and plants, or
oils made from those plants, that resonate most with you for well-being

or spiritual protection. I have experimented for many years and use a small variety that I know work well for my purposes. If I want to cleanse negative energy in my space, I use rosemary. If I want to bring peace and calm, I will use lavender, amber, or sandalwood. These are just the ones I use for spiritual matters, as opposed to health. Over time, I have observed the properties of these herbs working and have a good idea of which ones have a consistent effect for myself and my clients. There's no such thing as the "best" oils—one person might experience luck with some, while others need a completely different variety. It's fun to experiment and see which help you most.

Sage Smudging

Traditionally, this is an indigenous practice of burning one of the four medicines—sage, cedar, sweetgrass, and tobacco—in an abalone shell to purify and cleanse any negative energy from a person or place. The shell represents the water element, the plants the sacred gifts from Mother Earth, the fire lights them all, and the smoke carried on the air represents the combination of the elements. The ashes left behind are said to have absorbed any negative energy. According to Eddy Robinson, Ojiwa cultural educator, "To prepare the room, cover mirrors, close windows, open doors (including cupboards), and turn off all electronics." After the room has been prepared, start on the left side of the room and circle the house or apartment you are cleansing, asking the good spirits to stay and the negative spirits to leave. Push the smoke out through the front door.

Saining

....

Saining (meaning blessing, consecrating, and protection) is the Celtic tradition of sacred smoke and uses mugwort or juniper. Instead of a bowl, an abalone shell is used. Traditionally—in Scotland, for example—"magic water" is sprinkled throughout homes and beds on New Year's Eve, and doors and windows are shut tight with juniper branches burning so that the home is filled with cleansing smoke. When the people in the home sneeze or cough, windows and doors are flung open to let the cold air in for the New Year. At that point, everyone celebrates with a bit of whiskey. Sounds nice, doesn't it?

If you want to do a milder form of cleansing (and/or you'd rather not fill your entire home with smoke), you can use a fire-safe bowl and some juniper. Light the juniper on fire, letting it burn for a moment before blowing out the flames. Pass the bowl around your body, an object, or your home to bless or cleanse it, making the sign of the cross in the smoke. To truly honor this tradition, remember that Celtic crosses are more X-shaped than the T-shape we normally associate with a cross. In ancient Scotland, this technique was used to bless a variety of things—they even sained their livestock!

Sacred Smoke

The Vikings used smoke during funeral rites, sending the deceased out on a raft, then shooting arrows of fire at it until it burned, sending them to Valhalla or heaven. The Christian Church burns incense to symbolize prayers rising to heaven. Taoists burn smoke with joss sticks or paper to send prayers, and also to purify evil spirits. It's universal to use sacred smoke. Here is a short list of herbs you can burn to create your own blessing or banishings.

- **African Violet:** for protection and to promote spirituality within the home.
- **Basil:** to exorcise and protect against evil entities (such as demons and unfriendly ghosts).
- **Clove:** to stop or prevent the spread of gossip.
- **Dragon's Blood:** for protection when spell-casting and invoking.
- **Fumitory:** to exorcise demons.
- **Galangal:** burned to break curses cast by sorcerers.
- **Mint:** to increase sexual desire, exorcise evil supernatural entities, conjure beneficial spirits, and attract money.
- **Rose:** to increase courage and induce prophetic dreams.
- **Rosemary:** to banish evil.
- **Sage:** for protection against all forms of evil.
- **Vervain:** to exorcise evil supernatural entities.

Using Essential Oils

You can also use essential oils to purify, bless, or banish. You can dab the oil of your choice on yourself, or an object on your altar, or you can put some in a diffuser. Here's a short list of oils that I like to use:

* Lavender: to calm and sooth, and assist prayers and blessings.
* Cleary Sage: for cleansing and banishing negative energy.
* Frankincense: for purifying yourself or a space.
* Orange: to bring joy and sweetness to life.
* Peppermint: to refresh, awaken, and clear your mind quickly.
* Rose: to reduce anxiety and loneliness, and bring love.
* Sandalwood: to bring us closer to the Divine.

CHAPTER 21

Light and Shielding

YOU HAVE PROBABLY HEARD PEOPLE SAY "LOVE and light" enough for one lifetime—that aphorism is repeated so often in spiritual circles that it can make your head spin. However, it's a phrase that represents a real practice when understood properly and not just repeated ad nauseam until it means nothing. Recall the chapter about cold, cluttered spaces that harbor ghosts and other entities. What is the antidote to this energy? It is pure warm light. If we are cold and step into a sunbeam, we warm up and feel life flowing back into our bodies. It is the same energetically with lower or darker energies—these aren't always a spirit or the deceased; sometimes it is just bad vibes in a place that is unhappy or angry. When people have too much negative energy and emotion around them or stored up inside them, they emanate a slower, lower, and darker vibration than someone who is healthy, energetic, and positive. And just to be clear: fake positive people are *not* in the light. Their energy is more like an artificial spotlight as opposed to pure sunshine, and this false cheer has a lower vibration too.

When I began to really see the darker, lower vibrations around me, I realized I was basically marinating in it—so many apartment buildings, workplaces, and even cities are full of darkness. That's why it's so important to pursue ways to find the light, even when you're surrounded by shadows. Too much dark energy—heaviness, depression, denial, anger, dissociation, confusion—can all accumulate in us if we're around it. We can become sick, tired, depressed, resigned, or apathetic unless we have techniques to combat its effects. It's all energy, after all; so if you're an empath and absorb it without knowing how to release it, you will manifest it in yourself. This may result in symptoms like ear or back pain, headaches, a lack of motivation, or pessimism and negative thoughts, and the longer you stay in that place, the more resistant to change and positive energy you may become. The light, by contrast, brings warmth, optimism, clarity, insight, gentleness, patience, compassion, and subtlety. To break free and cleanse our lives of the darker vibes, we must process our emotions and change our lives to become healthier again. We may need to move, quit a job, detach from a relationship or two, rein in addictive behaviors, eat healthier, exercise more. The trajectory of becoming healthy in all ways is a process; and while it may sound magical to let the light in, it's half and half: one part individual agency and one part universal intervention. To me this means we can't heal in a vacuum. We set changes in motion with our actions, and we can also help ourselves change in more graceful, easier ways if we also work with the light.

When people come to me with a negative energy attached to them, or they are in a bad state of mind, I know there are people or situations in their lives that carry this darker energy and manifest these lower vibrations. Sometimes the people who come just need support and to talk, but other times they need an entity removed or a relationship cord cut in order to feel set free so they can feel the light around them. Every time I have encountered a person who is married to, dating, or working with a narcissist, sociopath, or psychopath, I see very dark energy around them. Clients in this situation may have difficulty even seeing light when it's shining on them—they may feel enveloped and trapped in this dark energy.

To counteract this feeling, I recommend visualization. Because people in this situation usually have a hard time seeing themselves, I ask them to imagine themselves sitting on a sunny beach. The light doesn't seem to shine on them, as if it eludes them; but I get them to keep thinking, searching for the sunlight. By using different metaphors to describe the positive energy surrounding them, they are able to eventually find it for themselves, a process that brings relief, elation, and freedom.

Whenever I get them to visualize the person or circumstance that is the source of this darker energy, I notice there are consistent features. People who are abusive will have no aura, no light around them. They always show up with a black or fuzzy gray void around them. When I ask the client to help visualize light around that person, they can't see it. It almost never works. The next stage is to ask them to look for connections or cords between themselves and that person or situation. When there is very abusive energy, there is never a cord. This energy hovers around the affected person, like a mosquito that sucks their blood and won't go away. That image may sound bizarre, but this is a consistent feature of visualizations I've seen over fifteen years. It is only by learning how to send an abuser's energy away, and by helping the client restore the light around them, that they feel relieved. Once they can really see light surrounding them, I ask them "Do you want this person in your life?" They always say *no*. Before we do this exercise, they always show up confused and still want to please their abuser. It's fascinating and also very sad that the pull of a toxic person creates such a strong dark aura that the healthy person they're affixed to loses the ability to perceive their own desires.

When people speak of the light, lightworkers, or being in the light, this is what they mean. It's a state where you can fully perceive that you are surrounded in divine light, love, and sunshine. If you can see this everywhere around you, then you are protected. If you can't see it at all, there is something or someone toxic around you. If you can see partial light and some darkness, then you likely have an etheric cord, an attachment, that must be removed. Try to meditate and visualize light around you as much as you can. This in itself is a protective practice. I do it before every mediumship session, every class I give, every past-life regression, every Reiki session. If I know I am in the light, I know I am protected, and the work and messages that come through are for the highest good and communicated to the best of my abilities.

Self-Healing with Light

I will let you in on something that can really help you if you get good at it: visualizing the light and allowing your mood and body sensations to shift. If you are able to do this, then you will be able to heal yourself with the light. This doesn't mean you shouldn't go to a doctor when needed—this technique won't protect you from common health issues. But it is useful for minor aches, pains, headaches, and of course emotional issues that can provoke these kinds of ailments.

You need to bring yourself into a deeply calm and meditative state for this to work. I'd recommend using the light-shielding exercise from pages 134–135 to get yourself there. Once you are fully able to see the light surrounding you everywhere with no missing areas, and are fully in this warm, wonderful light, you can allow that light to enter your body. So, if you have a sore back, you can visualize the light everywhere around you like an aura, then imagine the light going into your back and filling all areas where you experience pain. As this visualization starts to work, you will feel the negative energy in your body start to release. Sometimes people have an emotional reaction and must allow that to come up. Bringing in the light will purge the pain, fear, or trauma that is held in your sore back. You can do this with any minor ache or pain and often find quick relief.

CHAPTER 22

Removing Negative Energy

W E ALL HAVE HAD A BAD DAY—STUCK IN TRAFFIC on your commute, fighting with friends or family, or stressed out by events at work. Daily life has its stressful moments; and when we leave work or school, we can bring home negative energy that poisons our mood. If it's a daily thing, it can weigh us down. Bad days are common—that's why it's good to know how to remove negative energy when it accumulates. Let's start with the easier techniques and work our way up.

If we are repeatedly in an environment or have to encounter toxic situations or people, it is even more important we learn to clear it and restore ourselves after we leave. It's one thing to feel heavy or drained sitting on the bus next to someone, and it is a relief when they get off at their stop. It's quite another to feel this way every time you are around your boss, teacher, or apartment building. There are many ways to protect ourselves and separate out what isn't our vibe to absorb and carry, or even feel responsible for. Let's start with the easier techniques and work our way up.

Banishing Bad Vibes

Remember a bad day you had recently. Choose something that wasn't traumatic or shocking, just annoying, frustrating, a bit of a bummer, or representative of some other mild form of bad energy. Sometimes even a simple frustrating interaction at a Starbucks can be enough for you to feel a slight stain on your day.

First, try to see yourself surrounded in beautiful, warm white light, or see yourself fully surrounded by sunshine on a beach. Can you see it? If you can, then call to mind the negative event or emotion of that day. See where it is situated around you. Maybe the Starbucks barista is standing right there in your space, or the person who cut you off on the road is close beside you visually. Now I want you to push that interaction back a bit in your mind, give yourself some distance from it. Is it working? Do you feel relief? Most people do when this works. If you want to, you can go ahead and see the barista or car shrinking into a small dot or disappearing in a flash of light. You might feel your energy shift at this point—a relief of muscle tension, your eyesight becoming clearer, a feeling that your head is back on straight. This is a great sign that you have removed this energy.

But what if this energy is persistent and harder to clear? What if you have a hard time seeing the barista or the car disappearing or shrinking down to a dot, or you have a hard time fully seeing the light when calling the sources of your negative feelings to mind? First, try bringing in stronger visualizations of the light. If you see that barista standing there, try flooding yourself in an even brighter light—whatever that looks like to you. Try visualizing something to help you push the barista farther away. Do you need to see someone escort them away from your presence? Do that now. Do you need to feel some other method that would give you the separation you need? For example, you could build a wall, see them get on an airplane and fly away, imagine a rope or a ladder appear for them to climb—whatever works for you. Remember, you are not harming them. These images are just metaphors for the energy that is sticking around you. Keep working with these techniques to see if something removes this vibe from your life and continue until you get relief. If that still doesn't work, we up the ante and cut the energetic cords.

CHAPTER 23

Cutting Energetic Cords

T HERE ARE ENERGETIC CORDS BETWEEN ANY
of us who have made a connection on some level. Many times,
these cords are good, and we want to keep them; but others are very
binding and harmful. Cords can look like anything from a tiny glowing
thread to a thick dead tree branch to a metal ball and chain. When you
visualize your energetic cords, the image you receive is a metaphor for
the quality of energy between you and the other person.

We can have cords to places as well. Perhaps you were not happy in
the city you lived in, so you moved to a new one. Things have started
well, but after the first few months you find certain patterns repeating
themselves, even if there is no good reason. For example, you used to
feel nervous walking home at night alone in your city, but now you live
somewhere very safe and friendly, but you still keep doing the same
things you did to feel safe walking alone. You might keep your head
down, avoid eye contact, and similar strategies. The thing is, it doesn't
make sense in your current location, so there might be energetic cords
tying you to your old city and those old habits.

Repeating habits and patterns that came into play with a certain person, job, or location, then repeating them when they no longer make sense can mean energetic cords are present. A happy example of this that might make it easier to understand is when you feel a lingering connection to a particularly amazing vacation you had, and your mind is always there. There is a positive-energy cord to that vacation spot. Not all energy cords are bad. Many of our love bonds are energetic cords that are positive. It's just a good idea to cut the ones that keep you from moving on with your life.

Whenever you feel truly stuck or can't stop your mind from rehashing some event or obsessing over another person's motivations, it can be useful to check for energetic cords. If the energy is a burden, you will feel a huge sense of relief once they've been cut. You'll also get some insight into your own life by investigating the cords that bind you. When they are cut, you'll often be able to see a situation with perfect clarity.

Cutting the Cord

Using the scenario from the last section, in which a chance encounter with a rude barista or an angry driver messed up your day, you can take it even further and cut the cords holding you to those events. Visualize it: Are there are any energetic cords to that barista or the annoying driver piloting the car that cut you off? Always feel the light around you first, then see in your mind's eye where the source of the negativity is in relation to you. If you want, you can check what mood the barista is in, or what kind of vibes the car and driver may be giving off, and also check whether you can see any light around these sources. Many sticky and stubborn energies don't have light around them, but you might see other colors or partial light—not all connections are purely negative or positive.

The first step is to create a comfortable distance between yourself and whatever you are connected to. Similar to the exercise in the last chapter, push them back a bit in your mind to where the distance is comfortable for you. Send the barista a few steps back. Make the car back up and the driver take his foot off the gas. Just as in physical reality, you will feel relief when the distance is sufficient. It might be six feet, or it might be a football field—keep adjusting until you feel your muscles unclenching, your anxiety dissipating. Check again and gauge the mood of your subjects and see if it has changed, now that you have set this energetic boundary. Can you see light around them now, or colors? Often when we reset this boundary, other aspects of the sources of negative energy get healthier when you visualize yourself in a safe place, although some will stay fuzzy gray or black no matter what you do.

At this point, you should check in to your visualization to see if there is any kind of cord, rope, branch, thread, spiderwebs, or any attachment between your body and the source of the negative energy you are investigating. Take a moment to really feel this link and see this cord clearly. Where does it attach to your body? How deeply? Where does it attach to their body? How deeply? Seeing where cords attach to locations on the body can tell me a lot about the kind of connection.

The next step is to be clear and sure that you want to cut this cord. At this point, I usually call on Archangel Michael to cut the cord with his sword of light. I call on Archangel Raphael to remove the roots of the cords from you and the other person. But there are many ways to cut energetic cords. You can simply visualize the cord being cut and pulled out at its source, releasing you both, and dissolving, disappearing, flying up into the light and back to the Source. If you want, you can call upon the Archangels to fill you with light in the places to which these cords and roots were once attached, asking them to restore your energy, healing you and releasing you for your highest good.

Allow yourself to really feel this shift, and rest afterward. Do your best not to start thinking about this person or situation again right away, or you are in essence reattaching the cords. Give your mind a complete break and do something enjoyable. Stay in the relief and in the lightness you now feel. This exercise is sometimes more effective with a guide or extra support such as a professional medium like me, and sometimes it needs to be done multiple times. It takes a lot of mental strength and self-discipline to stop thinking about a person or situation that has done you harm, but you must continue to process your deeper feelings and allow the truth to emerge about your situation. Cutting cords can help you start feeling space to do this and does have an effect of breaking the hold this event or person has on us.

Cord-Cutting and Physical Healing

....

I once had a client come to me because various things in her life were not going as she wanted, and she felt she needed Reiki to help rebalance her energy. She didn't expect that during the Reiki session I would sense the physical pain she was having in her hip. She was more focused on her current life decisions and a general feeling of being stagnant. But when I began to do Reiki on her body, I saw an energetic cord attached to her hip that was causing her pain. I asked her if she wanted to explore this and cut it. She assented right away.

As I asked her to surround herself in light, then visualize the cord right where she had her hip pain, she described it looking like a strong tree branch, made of solid wood and immovable. I guided her to look at the end of this cord and see if it was attached to anything on the other end. She got emotional and said her father was at the end of this cord. I asked her where this cord was attached on his end if it was, and she saw it coming from his stomach. I explained the meaning of the cord originating in his stomach. Generally, cords attached to stomachs might mean there were ego or control issues at play. My client immediately said, "Oh *hell*, yeah." I asked her if she wanted to cut this cord, and she of course said yes. I once again guided her to visualize her light and then use anything she wanted to sever the cord between herself and her father. I told her to see her side of this cord removed gently from her body, allowing it to separate visually, and then asked her to let me know how she felt. She felt a relief in her hip right away. We then removed the cord from her father and sent that energy back to the light or Source. I then guided her to visualize that same beautiful light entering her hip and filling up every part of her body where the cord was, and she felt a huge relief. She told me about two months afterwards that the pain in her hip had never come back.

Cutting Cords with Narcissists and Sociopaths

These are special cases where cords are really hard to cut. Why? Because every time I have done a session for someone dealing with a narcissistic or sociopathic person, there is *no* cord at all. There is gray static, fuzz, or black energy all around this person, but they are not corded to the people they affect. Their energy hovers around their victims and sticks like noxious smoke. Typical cord-cutting in the way I described previously just doesn't work.

So, what do we do in this case? What I have found to work is once again asking the affected person to envision their light, then bring this person to mind. I ask them to see where the person who is causing them pain is located in their mind. Most people will tell me that that person is standing behind them, or so close to them it's uncomfortable—sometimes right in their face. This is typical of a controlling person.

The first thing I do after that is ask my client to visualize the narcissistic person standing back at a comfortable distance and facing them, not behind or on their side. I then ask them if this person's demeanor changes when made to face them and respect them by giving them distance. Usually, the person they are visualizing will look either angry or depressed. I then ask them if there is any light or color around this person's aura. They will always tell me no. It's black, gray, static, or fuzz. I ask them to try poking a hole in the gray or fuzz to see if any light wants to come through. For some, this works, but most times it doesn't. I ask their permission to remove this person, and it's always a yes.

Next, I guide them to visualize this person backing up or shrinking into a little dot. This is almost always a profound moment for my client. They might let out a huge sigh, their heart might calm down, their body sinks in or relaxes finally, or they need to cry. There is always relief. When I ask them if they want this person to come back into their lives, they always say no. If this person was an intimate partner, they usually realize they were not in love, they were *preoccupied* with this person— they were scared to say goodbye or set boundaries with them. It was never my client who was not over it or not clear about their needs. This exercise helps them realize how uncomfortable it is to have someone hover over you or stick to you without any heart attachment.

Having a narcissist or sociopath in your life is a feeling of being the mouse to their cat. You can't stop thinking about them not because of love, but because of hypervigilance. I have found this pattern really fascinating, and very consistent over many years.

Cord Attachments and Meanings

Heart to Heart

This is a definite emotional or familial connection if you see a cord from your heart to theirs. To know the quality of those feelings, though, you need to assess what that cord looked like. Was it a metal bar? Was it a golden ribbon? Was it made of wood? Was it made of light? Does it look thick or thin, long or short, healthy or broken? All of these are metaphors for the health of that heart connection.

Heart to Head

In this instance, the person with a cord connecting to their heart has an emotional or romantic connection, while the other's is attached to their head, their ideas, or intellect. So in this case, one person is emotionally available and attentive (the one with the cord attached to the heart), while the other is thinking, analyzing the bond, or has become emotionally detached. This is usually a painful imbalance.

Heart to Genitals

I often see this dynamic in imbalanced couples in which the person with a cord connecting to the heart wants love and the other is primarily concerned with their sexual attraction or needs. While it feels good for a while to be desired, the relationship in this case will eventually fall short for the person connecting from the heart.

Head to Genitals

Many people are corded at the genital level. I wouldn't bring it up twice, but there you have it! If the "head" person in this dynamic is always detached emotionally or overanalyzing things, and the other is wanting a sexual relationship only, this is also going to be a painful or shallow bond, but some people might find it comfortable and it often lasts longer than you'd think. Neither is involving their hearts, so the relationship may or may not endure; but it won't be love, that's for sure.

Other Combinations

Other weird body-part connections can happen with cords, and you can always use body symbolism to figure out the message. For example, if there is a cord from my knee to someone's mouth, one way to interpret this is that someone's words may be hurting me. The knees represent the need for forgiveness and sometimes point to bullying experiences. If there is a cord from my shoulders to someone's heart, we could see if the shoulder person feels somehow responsible for the heart person's feelings. This might be a sign of a relationship based on obligation or duty.

Interpretation is endless but rich, and the process of decoding the symbolism when it comes to cords can be intensely revealing and enriching. This is another situation in which working with a professional medium can be helpful!

Part 5

Grounding It into Daily Life

A LL OF THE EXERCISES AND INFOR-
mation in this book may feel overwhelming
to digest and bring into your daily life, so how can
we start integrating these practices and concepts?

First of all, it's really important to honor your
energy level and capacity to take on new things at
any stage of life. Sometimes we're ready to learn
big chunks of new information or change our habits immediately, but sometimes it's better to take
teeny steps. Be honest with yourself for a moment.
What struck you most as you read this book so far?
This is your intuition calling you to that area first.
If you got excited about the dreams section, you
could start by keeping track of yours in a daily journal or adding accents to your bedroom or routine
to improve your sleep life—new bedding, a scented
candle in the room, bedtime rituals to prepare
yourself for the dream world. If you were most
excited about the animal totems, you can write
down the animal dreams and encounters you've
had in your life so far and look them up to decode
what they mean. You can journal about them and
find things to bring the animal spirit that resonates
most with you into your space—even if that just

means placing a stuffed toy bear on your book-shelf. If the animal totem is your strongest guide, you can watch documentaries to learn more about the nature of yours. If the section about altars and sacred spaces hits home the most, perhaps you can create one and enhance it with beautiful and meaningful objects. You can create a code of conduct for your space and tune in to whether you want this to be solely yours or a place where others can visit.

There is a lot to take in, and there is no hurry or deadline to try any of it. Let your intuition guide you and show you where to begin.

CHAPTER 24

Commemoration

I F THIS BOOK HAS INSPIRED YOU TO CONNECT WITH a loved one or a spirit guide, you can choose to perform an act of commemoration to that loved one or guide. It can be super-simple or as elaborate as you wish. You can use oils, such as those suggested on page 143, or sacred smoke to consecrate a space. You can read a letter or poem written to your loved ones or your guide. You can plant a tree in their honor, particularly one with a symbolic significance that corresponds to the energies of the one you are commemorating. You can make a beautiful meal and commune with them. It's totally up to you, but an act like this can be very meaningful and signal a new chapter in your life.

The more personal you make it, the more special it will all be. What is a detail of the person or being you're commemorating that has a story behind it? What playful ways can you express a part of their personality? What is something only you would know that you can represent symbolically? Let's find creative and heartwarming ways to commemorate the light in your guides and loved ones.

You might find these next examples inspiring.

Inspiring
Commemorations

Here are a few examples of wonderful ways to commemorate loved ones. It can be as simple or elaborate as you'd like, and each act is highly personal. Try some of the rituals mentioned here, or make up your own.

A PARTY FOR HER MOTHER

I recently spoke to a woman who lives near me as she was unpacking an impressive amount of groceries from her car. I asked what the occasion was, and she told me she was having a big party to commemorate her mother, who passed a year ago. The woman asked friends to come over and cooked all day so her many guests could eat well, listen to music, and dance. She had journals printed with the beautiful photos her mother had taken and gave each guest a copy. It sounded like a joyous way to come together with all who missed her.

A WOLF DREAM

Thomas had long worked on connecting to his animal-spirit guides; and when a strong presence of a wolf finally came through, he was elated. After that first contact, he dreamed of wolves, heard them in the woods off in the distance where he grew up, and started to study their symbolic meaning. For many months, he reflected on what his totem meant for his life at that time. This experience was so sacred to him that he decided to commemorate the date of his first wolf dream as an anniversary every year after, to remind him of the wolf's teachings.

He went to a local powwow and asked a craftswoman there if she had anything to represent the wolf, explaining his totem experience. The woman offered him a necklace with a wolf's tooth on it—an actual tooth, not just silver jewelry. He has worn this necklace ever since, and he marks his anniversary every year with a period of solitude in the woods, as well as donations to local charities that help take care of the land on which the wolves live.

GABRIELLE'S FAIRY HOUSE

Gabrielle was studying fairies in her paganism classes and had a strong vision of one in particular. This fairy was bashful at first, then silly, then willful. Gabrielle became enamored with this vision and the energetic, playful, clever demeanor of this fairy. She wanted to show respect to the creature, and so decided to commemorate it by dressing in white diaphanous robes and doing spins, dances, and jumps that looked like flying. She created a tiny dwelling for her fairy and gave offerings of food and candy. The energy the fairy brought into her life was vivacious and gave Gabrielle uplifted momentum to reach her goals.

CHAPTER 25

Journaling

J OURNALING AND WRITING ARE A GREAT WAY TO detail your spiritual journey. Any time you feel you've received an insight, a memory, or a message in some form, you can keep it in a special journal. I realized a few years after I had connected with my own spirit guide that my diaries from twenty years ago showed that I had dreamed of him already—before I even knew I had one. His description and personality were consistent. When we write down the details of our days, we don't always know what will end up being quite significant down the road, which is all the more reason to keep a journal. It also just helps us process a lot of the emotion that comes with this level of deep work.

Keeping your private thoughts and feelings in a diary can also be like creating an altar or consecrating a sacred space—it is another place to honor our experiences. If you are going through a difficult time, it really helps your healing process. If you are grieving a loss, it can also be a good place to sit with the feelings you are having and memorialize the person—and if that person is connecting with you in some way, you can write down all the details of that contact. Over time, if you write down any encounters or dreams you've had about your guides or loved ones, you will be able to go back and see patterns in your journal, and that will be a great comfort when you see that consistency emerge. Here is a simple way to organize your journal:

Exercise for Recording Your Contact Experiences

I always like to write the date and time so I can see over the years how far back things go, and also if there seem to be times of the year when I get more messages or dreams.

Write a detailed version of the experience, even if it feels weird or the details make no sense. They might become clearer over time.

If you'd like to try to decode the experience you've had, you can write a separate paragraph on your own interpretation. Leave space to write further thoughts at different times in the future. Perhaps you'll write your thoughts the day you received a message from Spirit but leave room to write down another insight about it a year later. The purpose of leaving additional space after each journaled experience is that you'll be able to see if your understanding has changed in that time.

This journal can also include different sections. One section might be the raw accounts of experiences you have had and their interpretations. One section might be just to record your dreams. Another section might be to record synchronicities, so you'll be able to look back at a running list of them. Organizing your journal in different ways makes it more fun to maintain and read, and can also be extremely helpful in increasing your insights later on.

Journal Exercise for Increasing Intuition

This is really basic, but it will be very life-changing. Every time you meet someone new, I want you to write out everything you perceive about this person. This account should be only a raw first impression. If you let yourself flow with it, you might pick up on a lot of details. Why? Because if you write down your first impression of a person, then gradually get to know them over time, you'll be able to verify your initial intuitive reading of them. This in turn will help you trust your abilities.

The second thing you should do in this journal is to write down as many examples as you can of situations in which your intuitive feelings in the past have turned out to be accurate. This can be a running list that you can turn back to when you need to feel the strength of your own intuitive powers and get a better sense of the mindset you were in when you had them. What helped you get into the flow of your own intuition? What blocked you?

And lastly, write down all the synchronistic experiences you have had—at least the ones you immediately remember. This will increase your awareness of them and can help you recognize more of them in daily life. Again, if you devote some time to this, you will see your self-trust increase, and it can also be a great way to understand the similarities in terms of where your mind was when you noticed the events you've recorded in your journal.

CHAPTER 26

Creating a Personal Sacred Space

A S JOSEPH CAMPBELL WROTE, "YOUR SACRED space is where you find yourself again and again." We already touched on sacred spaces a bit, but let's put that knowledge into practice. I've been in many homes as a professional medium, and whether they're of average size or sprawling mansions, it's not uncommon to find that at least one person living in the dwelling has no space of their own. One thing I often see is a married couple in which the woman has no room, or even part of a room, for herself. It's true that personal space can be a luxury for many, but not having somewhere that is ours and respected has its consequences. Do you know what this does to your self-worth and identity? It's not good, right? It's very important for everyone to have some claim to a spot—a table, a mantle, a windowsill, a corner of a room, an entire room, a tree, a pond, a yard—something, no matter how small, needs to be yours and yours alone. We all need somewhere that is sacred to just us.

As much as we may complain about—or even disdain—materialism, and even though this is a book about spirits, I believe we all need to accept that we are living in the material realm in a physical body, and ownership in some form goes with that. With ownership comes a sense of responsibility, pride, and accountability—even if it's only a small object or area. It starts with the small and moves up to something bigger or more encompassing. Owning your sacred space, and returning to it, help ground you and remind you of who you are and your mission, your values, and your goals. This level of staying connected to yourself is essential.

What can you put in your sacred space? What makes it sacred to you? For example, you can include a candle; a piece of nature like a tree branch, a rock, or flowers; meaningful photos or jewelry; or simply a cup full of water to symbolize emotion, abundance, or tears. You can add an essential oil or herb that calms or helps you feel centered. Add anything that represents you as your best self. You will need a degree of privacy if you can get it, and ideally some quiet so you can sit and connect.

What do you do in your sacred space? The answer is: anything. Anything that soothes your nerves, reminds you of your true values, helps you re-focus or commit to your goals, or gives you a sense of protection and light. You can meditate, write, read aloud, pray, or sing. This is your space, so do with it what you will!

Sacred Space Examples:
Which One Speaks to You?

1. A sunny room in your home with a yoga mat, meditation cushion, small sound system, plants, and books that inspire you.

2. An altar in your room with a velvet cloth, gemstones, certain jewelry belonging to someone special, candles, seashells, photos, a diary, and a bowl for incense.

3. A bench beside a tree in your back yard. You can bring the same picnic basket every time with tea, cake, and poems to read to the person you miss.

4. A walk-in closet that you transform into a magic space, filled with colors that inspire you and fabric that makes you feel protected, statuary and art of your spirit guide or totem animal, a collection of objects you've found that pertain to your guide or messages left for you, a Tibetan bowl, and palo santo wood for atmosphere.

The variations are endless, so really visualize what *sacred* means to you. If that space is devoted only to your spiritual development, what does it look like? Sound like? Smell like? And what things do you do in there? Are there special dates or lunar cycles you will celebrate or pray here? Brainstorm on this inspiration—how you can create this for yourself and start the process on a practical level. A dedicated practice will ground your spiritual life into daily life.

Bach Flower Remedies

Another wonderful thing you can do for healing yourself in creating a sacred space is to use Bach Flower Remedies. Dr. Bach was a British homeopath who discovered that certain flowers and plants had healing properties. He extracted material from the flowers and created tinctures for people to take by placing a droplet under their tongue.

Each flower has unique emotional healing properties, so they can be great for consecrating your space or healing on an emotional level. You can take the remedy you feel fits you best, or you can put a drop of it in your sacred space. You can also use Bach Flower Remedies for pets by putting a drop on your hand and petting them, or adding a remedy to your pet's water bowl. They're also good for children: you can add some to a child's bath, for example. I've had these remedies for years to self-heal and to clear spaces emotionally. If you'd like to see a full list of the thirty-eight remedies, you can go to the official site at www.bachflower.com.

CHAPTER 27

Removing Blocks to Mediumship

MEDIUMSHIP EXPERIENCES AND ABILITIES ARE available to us all, but many people have mental or emotional blocks that stop them from happening—and that's okay. Blocks will happen with anyone, even the most accomplished medium, but there are always ways we can mitigate their effects. I want to share a few things I've noticed that can get in people's way of developing or experiencing direct spiritual communication themselves.

Grief and Fear

Two of our most difficult emotional states to manage are grief and fear. Just know that the intensity of these emotions is enough to block—or make it very hard to hear—your intuition, inner voice, and therefore your guides or loved ones. If you're not getting the messages, dreams, or connections to Spirit you desire, I would start by getting some help with these emotions and then the rest will flow easily as you're ready.

Shifting Paradigms

As you encounter your core beliefs about life and death, you will need to be as honest with yourself as possible, even if it scares you. First of all, if you open yourself up to the belief that the soul survives death and can communicate, or even reincarnate, you will never be the same again. It may shake the religious teachings you grew up with, or it might fly in the face of your skeptical side that might think this is all there is—you die and then you push up daisies. If ideas about reincarnation, different realms of the soul, or the vast number of ways Spirit can speak still throws you for a loop, you will need time to wrap your head around these concepts and accept that they can happen before you will be able to receive any communications.

Your current paradigm got you this far in life and helped you survive. Your understanding about reality likely kept you stable, and in many ways certain beliefs about the soul, life, and death that underpin every religion or philosophy are what keep the fabric of a society together. Challenging this can be scary for us personally and for those close to us who see us changing. You have to give yourself lots of time and patience as you shift. You might encounter some big emotions along the way, whether they're grief or elation. It's like you're cracking yourself open and are flooded with light and high vibrations—things seem more connected and synchronistic, and layers of change and healing will happen faster. If the people closest to you are also open to these phenomena, then the transition to your new paradigm will be easier and your abilities to communicate will be much faster. Otherwise, you'll need to negotiate your relationship with those who doubt and make sure that you are unaffected by judgment or skepticism, either your own or from the people around you.

As you change your perception and open yourself to other belief systems, you'll develop spiritually. You will have more openness, more compassion, and more curiosity about this great mystery called life. I sincerely hope this book helps you on your path and supports you in following your heart on this spiritual adventure.

Conclusion

MEDIUMSHIP AND SPIRIT COMMUNICATION IS AS old as time and is available to all of us. Knowing and experiencing for ourselves that there *is* an afterlife, that the soul survives physical death, and that beings from other dimensions, past lives, and our own ancestors can be present and speak to us are a huge comfort to the psyche and can even give us a raison d'etre, an answer to why we are here. Shifting your paradigm to include these mystical—yet very human—experiences gives your life new meaning as to why you are going through your life lessons, why you have chosen certain family members or partners, and how you can be closer to the natural world as well as the supernatural. Everything is interconnected on all levels, lives, and realms. The more you trust this, and trust your own intuition in the process, your awareness of that interconnectedness will greatly comfort your soul, reassure you, and show you that you've never really lost anyone who has transitioned to the light.

Thank you for reading my book. I wish you peace.

Catharine Allan

Notes

CHAPTER 1

Page 5: *As* Atlas Obscura *reported:* Natalie Zerrelli, "The Hidden World of Tenement Fortune Tellers in 19th Century Manhattan," *Atlas Obscura*, December 4, 2015, https://www.atlasobscura.com/articles/the-hidden -world-of-tenement-fortune-tellers-in-19th-century-manhattan.

Page 10: *in the words of renowned anthropologist Professor J. J. M. de Groot:* Yammi Chinnuswamy, "Everything You Need to Know about Chinese Spirit-medium Worship," SMU, December 15, 2014, https://news.smu .edu.sg/news/smuresearch/2014/12/15/everything-you-need-know -about-chinese-spirit-medium-worship.

Page 12: *Kardec coined the term Spiritualism:* Allan Kardec, *Book of Mediums*, Paris: Didier et Cie, Libraires -Editeurs, 1861.

CHAPTER 2

Page 14: *As Rebecca Rosen wrote in an article:* Rebecca Rosen, "What Is a Medium?" Oprah.com, accessed September 17, 2021, https://www.oprah .com/spirit/what-is-a-medium-rebecca-rosen.

Page 15: *"Mental mediumship . . . occurs through the medium's own consciousness":* "Mediumship," The Arthur Findlay College, accessed October 28, 2021, https://www.arthurfindlaycollege.org/subjects /mediumship/.

Page 16: *Physical mediumship "can be defined as physical manifestation ...":* www.arthurfindlaycollege.org.

Page 18: *What is a trance? Cambridge Dictionary*. https://dictionary
.cambridge.org/dictionary/english/trance.

Page 19: *In* Seth Speaks, *we learn about Jane Roberts*: Jane Roberts, *Seth
Speaks: The Eternal Validity of the Soul,* San Rafael, CA: Amber-Allen
Publishing, 1984.

Page 20: *A perfect example of this:* Brian L Weiss, *Many Lives, Many Masters,*
New York: Simon & Schuster, 1988.

CHAPTER 3

Page 34: *If you read my first book:* Catharine Allan, *A Little Bit of Intuition,*
New York: Sterling Ethos, 2019.

CHAPTER 16

Page 125: *According to* The Irish Times: Steve Lally and Paula Flynn Lally,
"Irish Gothic: Fairy Stories from Ireland's 32 Counties," *The Irish Times,*
February 20, 2019, https://www.irishtimes.com/culture/books
/irish-gothic-fairy-stories-from-ireland-s-32-counties-1.3799341.

CHAPTER 20

Page 140: *According to Eddy Robinson:* "A Definition of Smudging," *Working
Effectively with Indigenous Peoples* (blog), Indigenous Corporate
Training, Inc., February 16, 2017, https://www.ictinc.ca/blog
/a-definition-of-smudging.

CHAPTER 26

Page 171: *As Joseph Campbell wrote:* Joseph Campbell, *A Joseph Campbell
Companion: Reflections on the Art of Living*, ed. Diane K. Osbon, New
York: HarperCollins, 1992.

Bibliography

Books

Andrews, Ted. *Animal-Speak: The Spiritual & Magical Powers of Creatures Great & Small*. Woodbury, MN: Llewellen Publications, 2002.

Campbell, Joseph, with Bill Moyers. *The Power of Myth*. New York: Anchor Books, 1991.

Cunningham, Scott. *Cunningham's Encyclopedia of Magical Herbs*. Woodbury, MN: Llewellen Publications, 1985.

DeBord, J. M. *The Dream Interpretation Dictionary: Symbols, Signs, and Meanings*. Canton Charter Township, MI: Visible Ink Press, 2017.

Devereux, Paul, and Ian Thomson. *The Ley Guide: The Mystery of Ancient Alignments*. New York: Thames and Hudson, 1979.

Edward, John. *Crossing Over: The Stories Behind the Stories*. London: Hay House UK, 2004.

Gawain, Shakti. *Living in the Light: Follow Your Inner Guidance to Create a New Life and a New World*. Novato, CA: New World Library, 2022.

Holland, John. *The Spirit Whisperer: Chronicles of a Medium*. New York: Hay House, 2010.

Hoff, Benjamin. *The Tao of Pooh*. New York: Penguin Books, 1983.

Kardec, Allan. *The Mediums' Book*. Scotts Valley, CA: CreateSpace Independent Publishing Platform, 2017.

Pinkola Estés, Clarissa. *Women Who Run with the Wolves: Myths and Stories of the Wild Woman Archetype.* New York: Ballantine Books, 1996.

Toy, Atala Dorothy. *Nature Spirits, Spirit Guides, and Ghosts: How to Talk with and Photograph Beings of Other Realms.* Wheaton, IL: Quest Books, 2012.

Weiss, Brian L. *Many Lives, Many Masters: The True Story of a Prominent Psychiatrist, His Young Patient, and the Past-Life Therapy That Changed Both Their Lives.* Palmer, AK: Fireside Books, 1988.

Websites

Robert Ohotto is an amazing Intuitive—here is a sample of his talks: https://www.ohotto.com/learn-what-chaos-cycles-are-and-how -they-affect-you/

John Edward is so clear and informative as a professional medium: www.johnedward.net

Lee Harris is another beautiful Intuitive I follow: www.leeharrisenergy.com

For the official site of the Bach Flower Remedies: www.bachflower.com

For more information on animal totems, Ted Andrews's site is invaluable: https://www.winddaughter.com/ted-andrews

Acknowledgments

ALTHOUGH I HAD NO TEACHERS FOR MY MEDIUM-ship gift, I do have many people to thank who contributed to my journey and development. I will not mention many by name, because they are clients, students, and friends who had true ability but do not work in the public eye, and I respect their privacy. Please know who you are and that your belief in me, sharing your own gifts as we confirmed and learned how Spirit speaks through each of us was instrumental and comforted me greatly on this path.

I also want to thank the spiritual store I worked in for so many years—the Melange Magique in Montreal, Canada. A huge thank-you to all the staff and community who created the safe space for all of this to happen for me and the many who came in for twenty-two years. We forget that anything esoteric—be it astrology, tarot, paganism, magic, and the many forms of spiritualism that exist—was still very taboo when the store was opened by Debra Aubin in the early 1990s. It was a courageous and bold business to run in the middle of a French Catholic city!

I would like to thank the role models I have never met—the professional and public mediums and intuitives who were out there teaching, showing their gifts, modeling what is authentic versus showmanship—John Holland, John Edward, and Robert Ohotto—thank you.

Finally, I need to thank my own spirit guides, who have been there all my life even when I was not aware or unable to hear them, just as is the case for us all. To my own ancestors who come through to speak—Grandma and Grandpa Thomas—and to the spirits of everyone who has come through to speak and help me help my clients find peace and closure, my deepest gratitude.

Index

About the Author

CATHARINE ALLAN IS A CLAIRVOYANT MEDIUM, intuitive, astrologer, spiritual coach, and artist.

She began to self-study astrology in high school and was having strong psychic experiences by her teenage years. Unfortunately, she grew up in a family where this was considered crazy, and didn't say anything to anyone until she moved to Montreal, Canada, and teachers and mentors started to appear in her life. In one of those "when the student is ready, the teacher appears" experiences, she found a number of mentors in the city at that time. Catharine began working with the tarot when she was twenty-two and started to read as a profession by twenty-eight. She was exposed to many spiritual paths while working in a metaphysical store for about thirteen years, where her abilities increased exponentially. She realized she was a medium only because the people she kept seeing in readings had passed on. Catharine has also had a lot of experience counseling and coaching people. She ran support groups for women, has done healing and Vipassana meditation retreats, and has studied and practiced sound healing, chakra cleansing, guided meditation, Reiki, Bach Flower remedies, gemstone work, and aura cleansing, as well as space cleansing. She also works with issues involving addiction, mental health, and forms of abuse.

She works with guides and Archangel Michael primarily. By night she has been a professional singer for an Italian wedding orchestra, a couturiere and costume designer (at one point sewing for the Cirque de Soleil), and in recent years has helped create and perform in local cabaret shows. She likes to craft, paint, sew, and sing, and believes art and spiritualty go hand in hand.

Catharine loves to help people develop their own abilities to trust their intuition and communicate with Spirit, so she offers some workshops and coaching programs, and gives one-to-one sessions. You can find all those resources and contact information here:

Website: www.river-rain.com

Special link for this book to take things further:
https://www.river-rain.com/vibes-from-the-other-side

Social Media

....

 https://www.facebook.com/riverrainspiritguides

https://www.instagram.com/catharine_river_rain/

https://anchor.fm/catharine-river-rain